Profitable Charting Techniques

Second Edition

Other titles in the *Millard on . . .* Series

Profitable Charting Techniques

Second Edition

Brian J. Millard

JOHN WILEY & SONS

Chichester • New York • Weinheim • Brisbane • Singapore • Toronto

First edition published by Qudos Publications, 1991

This edition © 1997 by John Wiley & Sons Ltd,
Baffins Lane, Chichester,
West Sussex PO19 1UD, England

National   01243 779777
International   (+44) 1243 779777
e-mail (for orders and customer service enquiries): cs-books@wiley.co.uk
Visit our Home Page on http://www.wiley.co.uk
or http://www.wiley.com

Other Wiley Editorial Offices

John Wiley & Sons, Inc., 605 Third Avenue,
New York, NY 10158-0012, USA

VCH Verlagsgesellschaft mbH, Pappelallee 3,
D-69469 Weinheim, Germany

Jacaranda Wiley Ltd, 33 Park Road, Milton,
Queensland 4064, Australia

John Wiley & Sons (Asia) Pte Ltd, 2 Clementi Loop #02-01,
Jin Xing Distripark, Singapore 129809

John Wiley & Sons (Canada) Ltd, 22 Worcester Road,
Rexdale, Ontario M9W 1L1, Canada

Library of Congress Cataloging-in-Publication Data

Millard, Brian J.
    Profitable charting techniques / B.J. Millard. — 2nd ed.
        p.   cm. — (The Millard on — series)
    Includes bibliographical references and index.
    ISBN 0-471-96846-3
    1. Stocks—United States—Charts, diagrams, etc.   2. Investment
analysis.   I. Title.   II. Series: Millard, Brian J. Millard on—
series.
HG4916.M55   1997
332.63'2042—dc21   96–47782
                                                              CIP

British Library Cataloguing in Publication Data

A catalogue record for this book is available from the British Library

ISBN 0-471-96846-3

Typeset in 10.5/12pt Times by Dorwyn Ltd, Rowlands Castle, Hants
Printed and bound in Great Britain by Redwood Books, Trowbridge, Wiltshire
This book is printed on acid-free paper responsibly manufactured from sustainable forestation,
for which at least two trees are planted for each one used for paper production.

Contents

Preface

The rapid growth in the use of personal computers and the ready availability of programs to manipulate stock market data has meant that interest in the charting of such data has never been higher. There is still, however, a certain mystique attached to the process by which a chartist arrives at a buying or selling recommendation for a particular share simply by a study of how the price has behaved in the past. There is also, among many investors, a disbelief that there is any connection between past and future behaviour of a share price. This book aims to remove the mystique from charting, and aims to show that there is a definite relationship between the past and future price movements of a share.

Although a computer will simplify the procedures discussed in this book, there is still room for the pencil and paper investor who marks prices of a small number of shares each week on graph paper. Such an investor is best served by the channel analysis method, which will provide an excellent forecast of the target areas into which the share price will climb or fall, and for which a calculator is not necessary.

Those investors fortunate enough to own both a computer and software to carry out calculations and plot the results have the advantage of virtually instant response to any commands to calculate and plot share price data. They can also select from a variety of ways of downloading share price data so that the task of maintaining a data base of share prices is simplified.

This book takes the investor logically through a consideration of the different types of chart and the various chart patterns which are encountered in these charts. An important aspect is the theoretical consideration of how these patterns follow quite naturally from combinations of cycles which are present in stock market data. Also covered is a discussion of the various indicators which can be used, especially the ever popular moving averages.

The fairly new technique of channel analysis is discussed in depth, and a taste is given of the even newer technique of cycle and probability analysis, which has only become possible with the advent of the more powerful personal computers of the last few years.

A constant message through this book is the partially random nature of share price movement. Because adverse trends can strike out of the blue, an investor is never more than about 70% certain that an investment decision is correct. Being 70% correct in buying and selling decisions should of course lead an investor to substantial profit over a period of time, but this only happens if great care is taken to avoid substantial losses on the 30% of occasions when the decision is incorrect. To this end, the book explains in detail how to operate a stop loss, and the final chapter is devoted to a set of rules by which the risk in stock market investment can be kept to a minimum.

Brian J. Millard
Bramhall

1

Introduction

The subject of technical analysis, i.e. the attempt to determine future share price movements by reference to historical data, is a vast one, covering many aspects from the plotting of charts to the calculation of extremely sophisticated indicators.

This book focuses mainly on charting techniques and the operation of a few powerful indicators, but with a chapter on the latest powerful predictive methods that can only be carried out with a computer. An investor can apply the principles discussed here by using only the simplest of tools: a pencil, ruler, eraser, pocket calculator and of course chart paper. A flexible curve or French curve that enables the smoothest curve to be drawn to pass through important high points or low points on the chart will be a useful addition. All of these items can be obtained from a High Street stationer. The investor who has a computer and a technical analysis package and the ability to print out charts will still need these tools, since it is useful to annotate such charts. Most packages cannot carry out channel analysis correctly; the flexible curve or French curve can be used instead. Charts used in this book, including those with channels, have been produced using the Microvest 5.0 and Sigma-p packages.

For investors who are new to the idea of stock market investment, it should be pointed out that this book does not discuss how to buy and sell shares, but does discuss methods which enable the investor to arrive at buying and selling decisions. There are a number of inexpensive books on the market which discuss how to buy and sell shares, what level of dealing costs are likely to be encountered, how dividends are paid, etc. *Stocks and Shares Simplified* (see Appendix) covers this ground in detail, as well as moving on to ways in which shares can be selected and moving averages can be employed to reduce the risk of entering the market at the wrong time.

INVESTMENT PHILOSOPHY

Before moving to a discussion about charting techniques, it is necessary to point out to the investor the importance of maintaining a logical investment philosophy. The most important rule of investment is to pre-serve capital. It therefore follows that a losing position must not be held in the hope that it will soon turn around, but must be liquidated as soon as it becomes apparent that it has turned sour. On the other hand, a winning position should be maintained for as long as it continues to gain. Many investors adopt the idea of a target level for the share price, selling once the price reaches the target. This idea of creating a target level for a share price, while useful from the point of view of crystallising one's expectation for that share at the outset, must not force the investor into a premature liquidation, leaving the share price to continue upwards without him.

The reader should now begin to see that the most important plank in the investment philosophy is objectivity. The investor who moves away from a purely objective approach is the investor who will start to lose money. It is not being objective to 'jump the gun' because a particular chart formation appears to be about to commence. The objective investor will always wait for confirmation, and thus avoid the many occasions when the chart for-mation does not proceed to fruition. Before making any investment, it is vital that the investor considers the potential for gain and the potential for loss, which are perhaps better described as the 'upside potential' and the 'downside potential'. Where these are not loaded heavily in favour of the investor, the opportunity should be left alone.

The investor should also avoid being too heavily focused on just a few shares. Such an approach will have the investor seeing chart formations and opportunities which are frequently a figment of the imagination. Since there are so many thousands of shares traded on the London market, then when the investor is at all uncertain about the message that the chart is giving, the motto should always be to look elsewhere for a more clear-cut picture.

One chart which it is always essential to maintain is a chart of a broad-based market index such as the FTSE100 Index. The behaviour of the market as a whole can act as a useful brake on a euphoric investor who thinks he has found Eldorado all in one share. While individual shares can and do buck the trend of the market in general, this tendency to opposite behaviour is almost always short-lived. An investor needs to be extremely cautious when the market is moving adversely, and should never be afraid to admit that he or she has made a mistake and cut short an investment under such circumstances.

MONEY MANAGEMENT

In line with the prime requirement to preserve hard-earned capital at all costs, it is necessary to spread the risk amongst a number of shares. The larger the number of shares, the smaller is the risk, while the smaller the number of shares, the greater is the risk. With too large a number of shares, the portfolio performance will tend towards boring, since the few sparkling shares will be unable to compensate for the many dull ones. With too few shares, the performance will be sparkling if the selections have been correctly selected. On the other hand the performance will be disastrous if the selections have not been correctly selected.

Thus as in most other things in life, a compromise is necessary between risk and reward. This author is of the firm opinion that about eight shares is an ideal number in which to maintain an investment. Of course, these shares are constantly changing as the investment conditions for each share changes, although it is unlikely, except when just opening a new portfolio, that the investor will be buying or selling eight shares at any one time. What will happen usually is that one or two shares will come to fruition, and the investor will be looking for new shares with which to replace them. Occasionally conditions will be such that new shares cannot be found. In such a case the money freed by share sales should be invested in a reserve, which should be a short term high interest-bearing account, until such time as new opportunities occur.

From time to time the investor will make a mistake with a selection, finding that it fails to make the anticipated advance. Naturally, the only course of action is to recognise the mistake and sell the share. In a typical situation, the cost of such a mistake will be of the order of 10–15% of the purchase price of the shares. About 4.5% will be necessary to cover the dealing costs of buying and selling, and the share will probably have fallen by about 5% to 10% before the investor realises that the share is not going to recover. Since only one-eighth of the capital is invested in such a losing share, the loss to the portfolio is one-eighth of the 10–15% lost by the individual share, i.e. less than 2%. Such a loss is relatively trivial, and will easily be made up by one good winning share.

Never be tempted to decrease the number from eight shares, and never be tempted to bias the investment heavily in favour of one particular share. The investment should be reasonably close to one-eighth of the available capital in each situation. Naturally, if one share does particularly well, it could come to represent considerably more than one-eighth of the value of the portfolio. When moving into the next share, try to maintain an even stance, committing if necessary part of the released capital from the previous share into the interest-bearing account. The position can be evened up when an underperforming share is sold which requires the capital for the next investment to be topped up in order for it to continue to represent about one-eighth of the value of the portfolio.

REALISTIC PROFIT TARGETS

Many investors, about to enter the stock market for the first time, have unrealistic expectations for the gains which can be achieved, year upon year. In a bear market, it is extremely difficult to avoid losses, let alone make any gains. In a bull market, many shares double in value over the course of a year, so that an investor with perfect timing of the buying and selling times should see a gain of 100% provided he has selected these particular shares. Most other shares will make more modest gains, perhaps of the order of 30–40% over the same period.

Taking an average view, therefore, an overall gain of say 30% after dealing costs during a year of a bull market would appear to be a more reasonable level to expect. During a bear market the investor may well be uninvested in shares since no opportunities may present themselves. In the money market, therefore, a gain of 5% or 6% per year may be the maximum obtainable. Life being what it is, most investors would be making a few investments during such a bear market, and most investors would lose possibly 10% due to the unavoidable effect of dealing costs (say about 4–5% for the complete buying and selling transaction) plus a loss of another 5% before any stop loss is triggered. Thus a more realistic view of the return during a bear market may be 0%. Since we have said that the return during a bull market is perhaps 30–40%, this means that for all types of market an investor would appear to be able to look forward to gains of 15–20%, year on year, from investment in shares. This figure would seem to be reasonable when set against the avowed aim of many institutional fund managers, which is to match the FTSE100 Index. It is easy to see how such a limited aim has arisen—it can be said that a fund manager has never lost his job because he stayed level with the market. The pressure comes when a manager fails to achieve the gains made by one of these indices. On the other hand, to be fair to fund managers, they have a great deal of money to invest, money which if applied to just a few shares would heavily distort the market. They also have to operate at as low a risk as possible. Of necessity, therefore, they cannot behave as the small investor would do, limiting investment to just eight shares, but have to spread their investment amongst a large number. This has the unavoidable effect of depressing the gain or loss towards the market average.

We can throw more light on reasonable expectations for stock market profits by looking more closely at the behaviour of the FTSE100 Index over the last 13 complete years. Admittedly, many shares have outperformed this Index over this period of time, but equally, many shares have underperformed it. After all, the Index reflects an average view of the market, and so it is a reasonable approximation to what the average investor might have achieved. This 13-year chart of weekly closing values of the FTSE100 Index is shown in Figure 1.1. The values of the Index at the beginning and end of each year from 1983 to 1995, and the highest and lowest values reached during each year, are given in Table 1.1.

These values can be used to calculate the gains made by investors who invested in a number of ways during the period. We could have an investor

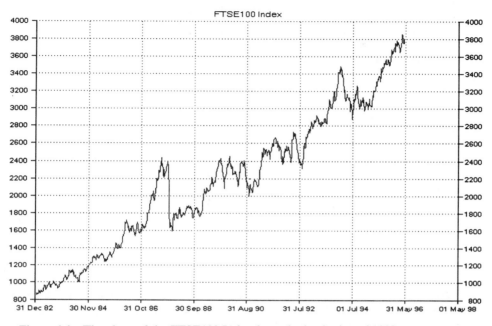

Figure 1.1   The chart of the FTSE100 Index from the beginning of 1983

Table 1.1   Values of the FTSE100 Index from 1983 to 1995

Year	Start value	End value	Year low	Year high
1983	864.8	1000.0	852.0	1000.7
1984	997.5	1232.2	986.9	1232.2
1985	1220.0	1412.6	1206.1	1455.5
1986	1420.5	1679.0	1370.1	1694.1
1987	1681.1	1712.7	1565.2	2443.4
1988	1747.5	1753.1	1694.5	1879.3
1989	1782.8	2422.7	1782.8	2423.9
1990	2434.1	2143.5	1990.2	2463.7
1991	2128.3	2493.1	2080.5	2679.6
1992	2492.8	2846.5	2281.0	2847.8
1993	2861.5	3418.4	2737.6	3462.0
1994	3408.5	3065.5	2876.6	3520.3
1995	3065.7	3689.3	2969.0	3689.3

buying at the beginning of the year and selling at the end of that year, or we could have an investor buying at the low point for that year and selling at the end of the year, or finally we could have an unfortunate investor who bought at the high point for the year and sold at the end of the year. The gains or losses made by these actions are shown in Table 1.2.

Table 1.2 Gains or losses made by three types of buying and selling action during each of the years 1983 to 1995

Year	Buy at beginning, sell at end	Buy at low, sell at end	Buy at high, sell at end
1983	3.6	5.6	−0.1
1984	23.5	24.9	0
1985	15.8	17.1	−2.9
1986	18.2	22.5	−0.9
1987	1.8	9.4	−29.9
1988	2.6	5.8	−4.6
1989	35.9	35.9	−0.1
1990	−11.9	7.7	−13.0
1991	17.1	19.8	−7.0
1992	14.2	24.8	−0.1
1993	19.5	24.9	−1.3
1994	−10.1	6.5	−12.9
1995	20.3	24.3	0
Averages	11.6	17.9	−5.6

In only two of the 13 years (1990 and 1994) did the market finish lower at the end of the year than at the beginning, with the average gain, taking all 13 years, for a year being 11.6%. An investor who correctly identified the low point for the year would have seen an average increase of 17.9%, while an investor who incorrectly bought at the high point for the year and sold at the end of the year would have made an average loss of 5.6%.

This helps to put the stock market into perspective, and shows that gains of about 20% year on year are realistic for an investor who is able to achieve fairly good timing of the buying and selling points for his shares. An above-average investor who is able to pick consistently the shares which outperform the market may make gains of up to 30% year on year, but such investors are scarce.

The impact of dealing costs on stock market gains should not be ignored. In very round figures, for a deal of say £1000, an investor can expect buying costs of about £25 and selling costs of about £20. This is equivalent to a total of 4.5%. For an investor who remains invested for long periods of time, more than one year, in a particular share, these dealing costs will be offset for the most part by the dividends which are received. It is the short term investor, who stays with a share for just a few weeks or months, who suffers most from dealing costs, since he is probably not invested in the share at the time when a dividend is due.

On the other hand, the short term investor gains markedly from the compounding effect of being able to reinvest the proceeds of one transaction immediately into the next. Even quite small average gains per transaction grow quite rapidly into large annual gains. This is shown quite clearly in Table 1.3, where the typical gain, after dealing costs, for transactions of

Table 1.3   Cumulative gains for increasing numbers of trades per year

No. of trades per annum	% Gain per trade assuming 100% rise over year	% Gain per trade adjusted for dealing costs	Cumulative gain per annum if reinvested
1	100.0	95.5	95.5
2	50.0	45.5	111.7
4	25.0	20.5	110.6
6	16.6	12.1	98.4
12	8.3	3.8	56.4

increasingly shorter time is listed, along with the equivalent annual gain for reinvestment of the proceeds of each transaction in the next one. It can be seen that gains after dealing costs of 3.8% for transactions lasting just a month still accumulate into 56% for the year. The table also shows that there is no substantial difference between an investor who buys and holds for a year before selling and the investors who hold for six months, three months or two months, since they all appear to achieve gains of between 90% and 111%. However, as presented here for simplicity in using round percentage gains, the table is biased in favour of the long term investor, who has been given a nominal gain of 100%, with the other gains being adjusted on a pro-rata basis of half of this over six months, a quarter over three months, etc.

In practice, a gain of 100% over one transaction lasting one year will be difficult to obtain, whereas a gain of say 30% over three months will be much easier. This is because of the way in which shares move; they tend to put on their gains over a short period of time. Shares go through periods where their rate of gain is quite high, periods where they remain more or less static, and periods where their rate of loss is quite high. This will become more apparent when we look at charts later. The effect of this behaviour is that the high rate of gain is usually compressed into about a three-month period. This is a good average length of time for which an investor should remain invested in any particular share, and with good timing and good share selection it should be possible frequently to capture gains of up to 30% in such a period. Allowing for the number of occasions when the timing is not good, an investor who has become an expert at charting techniques should be able to make a gain of about 15% over each three-month period during good market conditions. When compounded into the next transaction, gains of 15% each three months become 74% over the year.

As stated previously, during bad market conditions the investor will be unable to do much better than the interest which can be made by putting his capital into the money market. Looked at in this way, the good gains which can be made during good markets have to compensate for the standstill position during bad markets.

THE USE OF A STOP LOSS

It might seem to be a rather negative approach to bring in a discussion of methods of avoiding losses at this stage of the book. After all, investment books should have as their objective the making of money through correct investment technique. This is of course the aim of this book, but it is an indisputable fact that more money is lost by investors who fail to sell at the correct time than is lost by investors who buy at the wrong time. All of the gains made by the correct application of the chartist techniques discussed in this book can be lost if the investor fails to act when the trend turns against him. It is therefore essential that the investor operates a stop loss system, and it is discussed this early in the book in order to bring home the overriding importance of doing this.

A stop loss is a price level below the current share price which the investor sets as the lowest point to which he is prepared to see the share price fall. A fall of the price below this stop loss must immediately trigger the investor to sell, with no ifs and buts. The stop loss method is therefore an automatic one, and the investor must not negate its use by sometimes failing to act on it because of a gut feeling that the share price will recover. All such gut feelings should have been taken into account when the stop loss level is originally set. The term 'stop loss' should more properly be called 'rising stop loss' since as the share price rises, the stop loss level is also raised, so that the price gain becomes built into the stop loss system. The stop loss should never be lowered.

The setting of a stop loss level is a balancing act between two basic requirements. Firstly there is the need to maximise the profit already built into the share price by virtue of a rise since the share was bought, which means of course that the effect of a fall has to be minimised. Secondly there is the need to avoid premature exit from the share which then may continue upwards without the investor. If share prices just went up in a straight line and then turned around and fell in an equally straight line, then the operation of a stop loss would be simplicity itself: the level would be set at a point fractionally below the current share price. Unfortunately, prices do not behave like that. Because of the existence of short term, medium term and long term trends, plus a degree of random movement, prices move up and down in zig-zags. If zigs are taken to be larger moves than zags, then the stop loss is intended to allow upward zigs to run their course, accommodate the downward zags, but protect against downward zags that turn into downward zigs. This is illustrated in Figure 1.2.

The crucial decision about a stop loss is the distance below the current share price at which to set it. If the level is set too close to the current share price, then the stop loss is triggered by a small zag in the price, so that the investor has then lost out on the succeeding rise (Figure 1.2, upper). If the level is set too far below the current share price, then the stop loss fails to be triggered until the zag has become an extensive downward zig, so

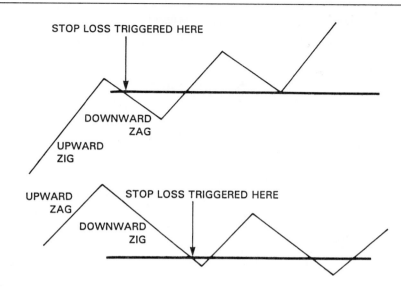

STOP LOSS TRIGGERED HERE

DOWNWARD ZAG

UPWARD ZIG

UPWARD ZAG

STOP LOSS TRIGGERED HERE

DOWNWARD ZIG

Figure 1.2 *Upper:* Stop loss set too close to the rising price gives a premature sell signal on a small downward correction. *Lower:* Stop loss set too far below rising price allows an appreciable loss to occur before giving sell signal. Note: zags are small price changes while zigs are larger price changes in either direction

causing the investor a loss that is much bigger than is acceptable (Figure 1.2, lower). The correct setting of the stop loss allows the investor to take in his stride the inevitable small downward zags in the share price, leaves him invested for the larger upward moves and makes sure that he is protected against a fall that is more than just a small downward zag.

There are two basic systems of stop loss which can be used. One of these is based on a floor which is a constant amount, e.g. 10 pence below the rising price. The other one is based on a floor which is a constant percentage below the rising price.

Constant Amount Stop Loss

The major advantage of a constant amount stop loss is that only the simplest calculation is required—subtraction. As the price rises, the constant amount is subtracted from the share price. Thus for a 10p stop loss, if the share price is at 340p, then the stop loss is at 330p. If the share price rises the following day to 345p, then the stop loss is raised to 335p. On the other hand, if the price falls, for example to 331p, then the stop loss stays where it is at 330p. If the price then falls to 329p the time has come to sell.

Thus the operation of the constant amount stop loss is simplicity itself. The real work comes in deciding whether the constant amount should be 10p, 12p, 20p or some other value. There is no requirement that the constant amount should be a nice round number such as 10p or 15p, and there is no relationship between the constant amount which is optimum for one share and that which may be the best for another share. A value such as 16.5p may turn out to be the best value for a particular set of circumstances.

The constant amount can only be determined by study of the past behaviour of the share price itself. The best way is to look at the chart of the share price and look at an upward trend which is reasonably comparable with the expectations you have for the current uptrend. Then make a note of the extent of each of the minor falls during the course of the extended rise. If the values lie close together, so much the better, since the constant stop loss may be acceptable if it is set at a value only slightly greater than the largest of these falls. There is more difficulty if the falls cover quite a range of values, since the larger of these may represent a fall which is quite unacceptable if the share price does not recover. Thus a compromise is often inevitable between the historical minor corrections in the share price and the amount of loss which the investor feels he can tolerate.

Having decided on a value for the constant amount, the investor should try this value on various parts of the share price history to see if the results obtained are satisfactory. If they are not, adjust the level slightly and try again.

Once the investor has carried out this process on a few shares, the experience obtained will make it much easier to decide on good values for other shares.

Constant Percentage Stop Loss

The world of investment is a world of percentages, so it is not surprising that many investors favour a stop loss system which is based on a floor a fixed percentage down from the rising price. I do not favour this method for two reasons. Firstly, the calculation is slightly more awkward than for the constant amount stop loss, especially as the floor level calculated will still have to be rounded off to the nearest whole penny or perhaps half penny. Secondly, a study of a large number of share price movements will show that the minor falls during the lifetime of a longer term uptrend tend not to increase in their value in pence as the share price rises, i.e. the falls are based on an absolute amount rather than a percentage amount. Thus it seems conceptually incorrect to use a percentage method for a share price movement situation which is not based on percentages.

As was discussed for the constant amount stop loss, the percentage value to be used can only be discovered by trial and error on the past history of the share price. For most shares, a value of around 5% or 6% will be found to give acceptable results, in the sense that the investor would not be shaken out of the share too frequently. Most investors would also be pleased to get out of a falling price only 5% or 6% down from the peak.

2

Charts and Indicators

In this chapter we will discuss the various types of charts which can be constructed and the simple indicators which can be calculated readily with the minimum of effort by the investor. The large number of more complex indicators, many of which require computer calculations, are more properly the subject of a wider ranging book on technical analysis. The chart types which will be considered are linear, semilogarithmic, point and figure, and rise–fall. The indicators which will be discussed are moving averages, the Relative Strength Index and the Welles Wilder Relative Strength Index. Each of these indicators falls into the category of calculated indicators, i.e. it is necessary to use the exact numerical values of the share price data at intervals such as daily or weekly to compute a numerical value for the indicator. The rise–fall indicator is a special case, since it is based on a trendline superimposed on the rise–fall chart, and thus needs no numerical computation.

LINEAR CHARTS

These are the simplest to understand and the easiest to plot. A linear chart has scales which are equally divided, so that a fixed distance along either the vertical price scale or the horizontal time scale is always equivalent to the same change in price or the same number of days or weeks of elapsed time. Before setting out to construct such a linear chart, the investor has to make two decisions. Firstly, for how long is the chart going to be maintained, and secondly, over what price range is the share price expected to move during the period for which the chart is going to be kept?

Linear chart paper as bought either loosely or in pads at a stationers will have two sets of graduations. The larger scale ones are heavy lines, and between these are fainter lines which represent divisions of tenths of the distance between successive pairs of heavy lines. The charts can be metric or imperial. In the first case the distance between heavy lines is one centimetre and between faint lines is therefore one millimetre, while for the imperial the distance between heavy lines is one inch and between faint lines one-tenth of an inch. Since an inch is approximately 2.5 cm, there are two and a half times as many lines in each direction on an A4 sheet of metric graph paper than there are on an A4 sheet of imperial graph paper. A metric sheet is usually ruled into a grid of 18 cm by 26 cm, giving 180 divisions by 260 divisions. An imperial sheet is usually ruled into a grid of 7.5 inches by 11 inches, giving 75 divisions by 110 divisions.

Which of these two types of graph paper is appropriate depends upon what the investor is trying to determine from the charts. For short term movements the metric chart will cover 110 days or weeks if the longer axis is used for the time. The larger separation of the graduations will make this type of chart easier to read, and for short term periods will possibly be the better of the two. The metric chart will keep the investor going for 260 days, i.e. one year if used for daily data, or five years if for weekly data, and therefore is more appropriate for viewing the bigger picture of share price movement.

Where the investor requires more thought is in the way in which the vertical price axis is to be labelled. The range should take into account reasonable expectation for the range over which the share price will move over the ensuing time period, and should include plenty of room for a fall from the starting point as well as enough room for a projected rise.

On the typical metric graph paper we have 180 vertical divisions, while on imperial paper there will be usually 75. The distance between heavy horizontal lines should be taken as a number which is readily divisible by 10, and not some awkward value which will make it less easy to plot intermediate values.

The major advantage of linear charts is their simplicity, since the same distance on the chart paper always represents the same difference in price or time. However, they do suffer from some disadvantages. Thus they do not allow the investor to compare percentage changes as easily as the semilogarithmic variety. They also do not accommodate unexpected surges or falls in the share price, which will then run off the top or bottom of the chart, necessitating complete redrawing to a different scale. On the other hand, as will be seen from the chapter on Channel Analysis, cyclical features in share price movement tend to be based on a constant amplitude, so that it is easy to draw channels of constant depth on linear paper. This becomes almost impossible on semilog charts.

SEMILOGARITHMIC CHARTS

Semilogarithmic charts have the same linear scale in one direction as linear charts, and since time is a linear function, then obviously the linear axis will be used as the time axis. It is in the vertical price direction that the two types of chart differ. The logarithmic scale has the property that a certain distance on the chart represents a constant ratio. Thus the distance apart of the points for say 100p and 200p on the price axis is the same distance as that between the points for 200p and 400p. Because of this, semilog charts have the useful feature that percentage change on them remains constant up the vertical scale. Thus if the underlying semilog grid is the same for the charts of two different shares even though the price marks on the grids may be different, then they can be directly compared from the point of view of percentage change at any moment in time. This is very useful where it is necessary to compare two investments.

One difficulty with logarithmic charts which limits their use with certain indicators is that zero and negative values have no meaning. They cannot be expressed on a logarithmic scale. For straightforward share charts this of course is not a problem.

Semilogarithmic chart paper has one further specification—the number of cycles on the logarithmic scale. This simply means how many times the scale runs from 1 to 10. A single cycle would have 10 heavy lines, getting closer together as they run up to the top of the paper. A two-cycle log paper would have the first cycle running from lines 1 to 10, the tenth being halfway up the paper, while the next cycle would start from line 10 and run up to another tenth line.

If the heavy lines are labelled with prices, then single-cycle paper would take the price up to a factor of 10 times the price marked at the first graduation, while two-cycle paper would take it up to 100 times. Naturally for share price movement, even a factor of 10 is usually excessive, so that single-cycle semilogarithmic paper will be perfectly adequate for share price charting.

As with linear scales, the investor will have to think carefully about the range to be used for the price scale. As stated above, it will cover a factor of 10 between the first and last values. The scale should start at a point comfortably below the current starting price in order to accommodate a fall in price without the necessity of redrawing the chart. If the current price is in the low 200p level, then 100p to 1000p would be sensible markings for the price scale. If the price is 500p, then 200p to 2000p would be obvious graduations to use. Note that the scale markings are multiples of the price at the first scale mark. Thus if this is 200, the next mark is 400, the next 600 and so on up to 2000. It is important to avoid numbers that cannot easily be divided by 10, since it will then be difficult to interpolate intermediate points on the fine grid lines. Thus 6, 8 and 16 are not good values, while 5 and 25, while not multiples of 10, are easily subdivided into 0.5 and 0.25.

Many commercial charts, on close examination, consist of small vertical bars. Often there is a small cross line horizontally through the vertical bar. These vertical bars are simply the range over which the share has traded during the day (or week for weekly charts). The lowest part of the bar is at a point corresponding to the lowest point, and the top of the bar of course is at the highest point. The cross line indicates the level at which the share price closed. Occasionally this might also be the highest or lowest price for the day.

For the amateur chartist, it is difficult to get at the daily range values without subscribing to an electronic feed of data to a personal computer. For this reason almost all amateurs plot just the closing price, or the closing price as it appears in the next day's newspaper. The point is plotted by drawing a line from the last plotted point to the current one. Such a chart is called a line plot, as opposed to the bar chart described above for daily ranges.

Examples of bar and line charts in both linear and semilogarithmic form produced by the Synergy TA package are shown in Figures 2.1 to 2.4. Note that movement is much less obvious in the semilogarithmic charts than in the linear charts because of the dampening effect of showing price changes as ratio changes as opposed to differences.

The chartist has the option of plotting daily or weekly values. Quite obviously there is five times as much work involved in daily plotting as opposed to weekly plotting. The best procedure is to carry weekly plots of the pool of shares which you are monitoring as the source of future investment opportunities. As a share approaches a point at which an investment opportunity seems imminent, then switch to maintaining a daily chart in

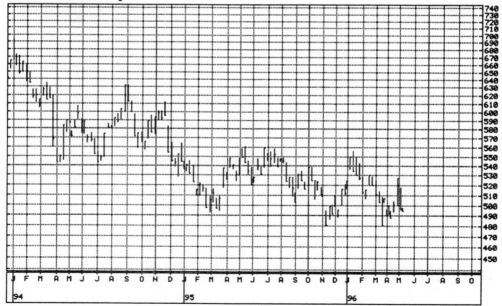

ALLD Allied Domecq

Figure 2.1   A weekly bar chart of the Allied Domecq share price on a linear scale

ALLD Allied Domecq

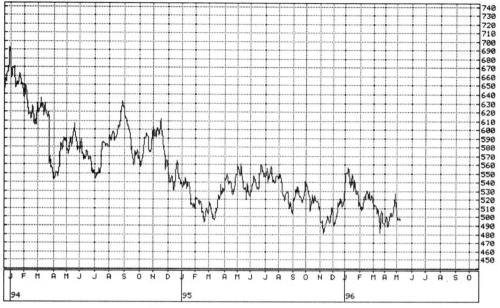

Figure 2.2   A line chart of the Allied Domecq daily share price on a linear scale

ALLD Allied Domecq

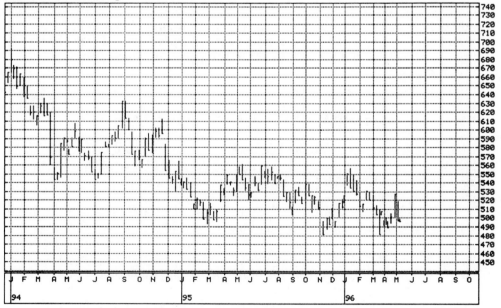

Figure 2.3   A semilogarithmic bar chart of the Allied Domecq share price

ALLD Allied Domecq

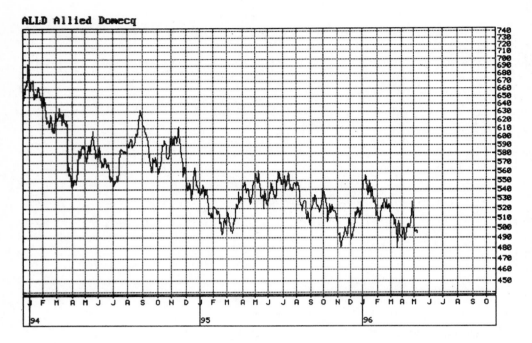

Figure 2.4   A semilogarithmic line chart of the Allied Domecq share price

addition to the weekly chart. In this way the amount of work is kept to a minimum. Note that daily charts should be kept for all shares in which you are currently invested, as well as those for shares in which you hope to invest shortly.

POINT AND FIGURE CHARTS

These are not as popular in the United Kingdom as they are in the United States. It is important that investors at least get a feel for what they mean, so they are described here so that investors will be able to construct their own if they wish.

The horizontal axis on normal charts is the time axis, and as such is equally divided into daily or weekly time intervals. Even if the share price remains fixed at a constant value for days or weeks on end, a point will still be plotted at the corresponding point in time. Point and figure (P&F) charts are quite different, since the horizontal axis is not a time axis. If the price does not change, no point is plotted on the chart. Because points are only plotted if there is price movement, P&F charts are a measure of the activity in the share in question.

Point and figure charts have a linear vertical scale, but unlike normal charts where a horizontal line corresponds to a price, it is the gap between the lines that corresponds to a price value in P&F charts. P&F charts are characterised by one further quantity—the box reversal. The most usual value is a three-box reversal, but the value can be anything from one box upwards. The higher the number of boxes the less sensitive is the chart to price movement. Hence the one-box reversal type is the most sensitive.

It is conventional, though not strictly necessary, to use Xs for a rising price and Os for a falling price. This makes it rather easier to read the charts. As an example, the way of plotting a one-box reversal P&F chart is now described.

The first thing to decide is the value of a box. This will depend upon the level of the share price. If the price is in the range of say 100p to 200p then a box could have a value of 5p. At the starting point in time, nothing will be put on the chart until the price has moved either up or down from that value. Supposing the starting point is 150p. Since the value of a box is 5p, the price has to move by that amount before any mark can be put on the chart. A movement of 4p up or down will not be plotted. If the price rises to 155p, or indeed any value between 155 and 159p, then an X is put opposite the 155p level. If the price falls by this amount, an O is put instead, but this time of course opposite the 145p level. Because the value of a box is 5p, the actual price movement is rounded to the nearest multiple of 5p downward for a rise and upward for a fall. For a rising price, Xs are put in all of the boxes up to that rounded value, and for a falling price Os are put in all of the boxes down to the rounded level.

We do not keep putting Xs and Os in the same column, since this would give little information about the share price movement. Since the type of chart being plotted is called a one-box reversal, we move to the next column to the right when the price movement changes direction. We put our X or O one box up or one box down from the previous last entry in the previous column. We still have to fill in boxes with either Xs or Os as appropriate up to or down to the new price level which is reached. For example, supposing the price has been falling so that the current column has a number of Os in it down to the box corresponding to 120p. If the price then moves up to 136p, we move one column to the right, put an X in the box corresponding to 125p (but not in the one corresponding to 120p) and then further Xs in the boxes for 130p and 135p. If the price then moves down to 129p, we move one column again to the right and put an O in the box corresponding to 130p. The result of these few moves in the price is shown in Figure 2.5.

When the price direction changes again we move again to the next column. We can now see that the greater the number of changes in the direction of the share price, the faster the chart creeps across the chart paper.

The one-box reversal P&F charts are too responsive to price changes to be of any great use in share price analysis. Because of this a three-box

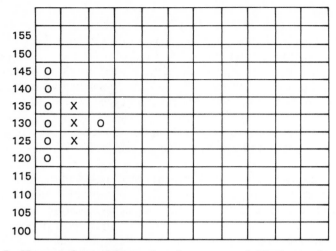

Figure 2.5 How a point and figure chart is constructed. The box and reversal size is 5p. Only movements of 5p or greater will be plotted. Price falls are represented by Os and price rises by Xs. Following a fall to 120p in the first column, a subsequent rise to 136p results in Xs being placed as shown. Finally a fall to 129p results in an O being placed in the 130p box

reversal is much more common. The principle is exactly the same as for a one-box reversal. You move to the next column when the price changes direction and by an amount greater than the value of three boxes. However, while the price is continuing in the same direction you continue to plot movements corresponding to one box. It is the reversal that has to be three boxes, while the continuation in the same direction stays at one box.

Reading Point and Figure Charts

Figure 2.6 shows the three-box reversal chart of BICC. The letters and numbers at the ends of each column give the month and the last digit of the year when the price reversal occurred. Thus A0 is August 1990. Trendlines can be drawn on P&F charts just as on normal charts, and two such lines are shown in Figure 2.6. The uptrend was broken by the long fall which occurred in August 1990. The downtrend line has yet to be penetrated on the upside, and so it appears that at the beginning of 1990 BICC shares were not yet ready for a rise.

RISE–FALL CHARTS

These are a third way of presenting share price data which is extremely valuable for determining changes in the direction of the share price which are signalled by penetration of trend lines.

BICC

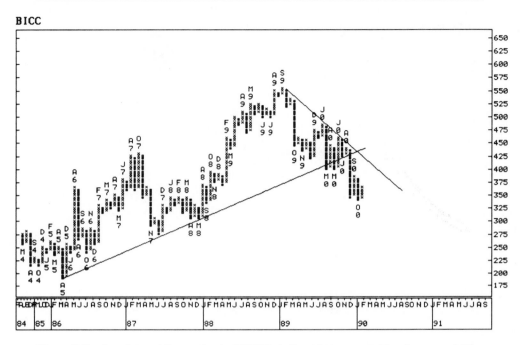

Figure 2.6 A point and figure chart of BICC. A three-box reversal has been used. The time of occurrence of reversals is indicated by the month letter and last digit of the year. Thus the latest reversal (into a rising trend) is in October 1990. As with normal charts, trendlines can be drawn as shown in this example

Normal charts have a price axis and a time axis, point and figure charts have a price axis but no time axis, while rise–fall charts have a time axis but no price axis. The vertical axis is a direction indicator, and its graduations are a measure of the length of time that a share price direction has continued.

It is the simplest possible chart to construct, and requires a linear chart paper. This is a case where the millimetric divisions on metric chart paper are probably too closely spaced, so that imperial paper graduated in tenths of an inch is much more appropriate. If metric chart paper is used, movement will be much easier to study if 2 mm graduations are used to represent one movement.

The horizontal axis should be marked as the time scale, either daily or weekly depending upon the lengths of trends which are being studied. Put the first point halfway up the vertical axis exactly on a horizontal line. For the next data point, if the price moves upwards, draw a line from the previous point up one graduation and across one graduation to the current date. If the price falls, draw a line from the previous point down one graduation and across to the current date. If the price is unchanged, draw a horizontal line from the previous point to the current date.

ALLD Allied Domecq Rise Fall

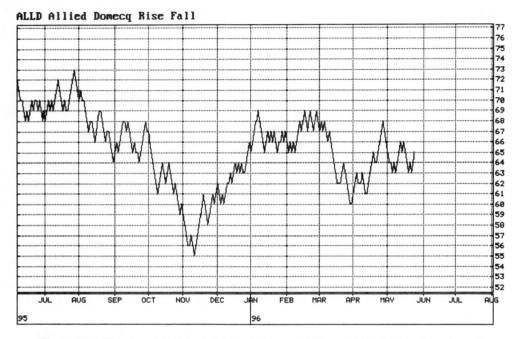

Figure 2.7 The rise–fall chart of Allied Domecq from mid-1995. The chart is constructed by taking an arbitrary starting number such as 100 and increasing it by 1 unit if the price has risen from the previous day, decreasing it by 1 if the price has fallen, and leaving it unchanged if the price is unchanged. Buying and selling points are determined by the breaking of trendlines

Thus the rise–fall chart takes no notice of the size of a rise or fall, but only that a rise or fall has occurred. An immediate picture is given of the length of time for which upward, downward or sideways trends persist. As will be seen later, the breaking of trend lines gives a very powerful method of early detection of the end of an uptrend or a downtrend. An example of a rise–fall chart is shown in Figure 2.7 for Allied Domecq.

NUMERICAL INDICATORS

Indicators are primarily used as an aid to the identification of the beginning of a new directional trend. Most indicators are numerical quantities that can be calculated from the share price data; others require some other source of data, such as the number of shares which rise or fall each day or week; and some, such as the rise–fall indicator, require only the addition or subtraction of 1 to or from a running total. The indicators discussed in this section are of the type which are easily calculated from the share price itself. They are very widely used, indeed in the case of moving averages universally used, and have stood the test of time.

MOVING AVERAGES

The vast majority of amateur chartists, and indeed many professionals, use moving averages without having the least idea of their mathematical properties. These mathematical properties are indeed very simple, but understanding them will bring a more objective approach to the use of moving averages in chart analysis.

Moving averages are 'better' representations of the share price itself. They remove what might be called 'noise' from the share price movement. The type of noise which is removed depends upon which span is used to calculate the average. The span is simply the number of points which are averaged. Thus a nine-day moving average is obtained by adding the prices for nine successive days and dividing by 9. The span of this average is 9. The term 'moving' is used because the investor moves through the available price data, continually adding up the last nine prices and dividing by 9. If there are, say, 11 daily prices available, then a nine-day moving average would have three values. The first nine prices when averaged give the first of these averaged points, the nine values starting with the second price and ending with the last price but one will give the second average point, and finally starting with the third price and ending with the last price gives the final, third, value of the moving average.

The above method of calculating an average is long-winded, and one can imagine the amount of effort required in calculating a 200-day moving average for say five years of daily data. The process can be greatly simplified by keeping a running total. How this is done for the Allied Domecq share price between 23rd February 1996 and 14th March 1996 is shown in Table 2.1 for a nine-day average. Five columns are required to carry out the calculation. The first column contains the date, the second the daily or weekly prices, the next column is a pointer to show which values to add to and subtract from the running total, the fourth column is the running total itself and the final column is the average, obtained by dividing the value in the running total column by the span of the average, in this case 9.

Adding up the first nine values gives a total of 4655. This is put in the fourth column on the ninth line down, i.e. in this case opposite 6th March. Dividing this by 9 gives the value of the average, 517.22, which is put alongside the total in the final column. Now to calculate the next value of the average, it is not necessary to add up a further nine values starting from the price on 26th February. Instead we add in the next price in the list, i.e. the tenth value on 7th March (512), and subtract the tenth price back from this point, i.e. the first value we used on 23rd February (520).

Table 2.1   Calculation of a nine-day moving average

Date	Price	Subtract	Total	Average
23/02/96	520	X		
26/02/96	519	X		
27/02/96	524	X		
28/02/96	525	X		
29/02/96	517	X		
01/03/96	511	X		
04/03/96	514			
05/03/96	512			
06/03/96	513		4655	517.22
07/03/96	512		4647	516.33
08/03/96	503		4631	514.56
11/03/96	508		4615	512.78
12/03/96	509		4599	511.00
13/03/96	502		4584	509.33
14/03/96	497		4570	507.78

This gives us a new total of 4647, which is put below the previous one. Dividing by 9 gives the corresponding average, 516.33, which is put in the last column. The use of the third column now becomes apparent. It is to enable you to remember which value has been dropped. Since the first value has been dropped, we put a cross in the first line in this column. The next time we do the calculation we will see that it is the second value which has to be dropped from the running total. Thus to the new total of 4647 we add in the next price of 503 and drop the price on the next line after the cross, i.e. 519, to give a new total of 4631 and a new average of 514.56. We then put our cross below the previous one.

We proceed in this manner until all the prices have been used up, so that we will have a running total and an average value alongside the last price in the list.

Obviously for averages with longer spans, such as 200-day, we will have much more work in calculating the first average value, but after that, we simply have one addition, one subtraction and one division to provide us with subsequent values of the average.

Note that Saturday and Sunday dates are omitted. Only business days, when the Stock Exchange carried out business, are used for the moving average calculations. There are differences of opinion on how Bank Holidays should be treated. Some investors take an average of the price before and the price after the Bank Holiday. It is best to put down the same value as on the previous working day, on the basis that a price stays the same until changed by the market.

We mentioned that moving averages remove noise from the original data, and that the type of noise removed depends upon the span of the average. A moving average will remove all fluctuations in the data with a frequency equal to or less than the span of the average, and allow through fluctuations greater than the span of the average. Thus a nine-day average would remove the random day-to-day variations in the share price and any fluctuations which are based on underlying cycles of movement which repeat themselves every nine days or less. Since variations of 10 days or upwards would still come through, a nine-day average is only moderately smooth, still showing the presence of short term, medium term and long term variations. In this context short term would apply to variations with a cyclicality of between about 10 and 30 days, medium term would apply to variations of between 31 and 200 days, and any variations over 200 days would be considered to be long term.

The values for spans which are used by various chartists can now be put into perspective. A 200-day moving average is common, and from the above comments we can see that its value is in removing short and medium term fluctuations, leaving the underlying long term trend visible. Thus it is sensible to avoid investment in a share when the 200-day average, and hence the long term trend, is falling. Also common are 10-day and 20-day averages, often used together, and here it is the short term and medium term trends that are being highlighted. These are appropriate to those investors who wish to take advantage of short term trends and who recognise the higher risk involved.

It is useful to keep two averages at the same time. In this case three other columns should be added to the table for each additional average: one for the subtract column, one for the running total for that average, and one for the average itself. Although as mentioned above, 10-day and 20-day averages are frequently used together, two averages are of much more value if they are much wider apart. Thus a 10-day average and a 200-day average can serve to throw light on both short term and long term underlying trends.

Plotting Averages on Charts

In Chapter 10, where moving averages are discussed, we shall see that averages are viewed as 'better' or smoother versions of the share price data itself. As such, they have to be plotted half a span back in time, which is the correct mathematical method of using them. However, the earliest chartists, who were in no way mathematicians, started plotting them incorrectly, and the practice has persisted so long that it is now not possible to eradicate it. The chartist way of plotting averages is with no lag, i.e. they are plotted exactly as they fall in a calculation such as that shown in Table 2.1. The value for an average is plotted at the same point in time as the last data point used for the calculation. Referring again to Table 2.1, this means that the average value of 517.22 would be plotted at the time corresponding to 6th March 1996. When plotted this way, movement of the average will lag behind movement in the share price, i.e. if the share price turns up from a falling mode, the average will take some time to respond and itself turn up from a falling mode. The larger the span of the average, the longer is this gap between the two events.

There are two basic ways in which averages are used in normal charting techniques. One method is to wait until the price moves above the average before buying and conversely wait until the price falls below the average before selling. The other way is to wait until the average itself changes direction. A reversal to a rising trend is a signal to buy, while a change to a downward trend is a signal to sell. The correctness of either method as a generator of buying or selling signals is extremely sensitive to the span of the average being used. Actual examples of the use of moving averages are given in Chapter 10.

RELATIVE STRENGTH INDEX (RSI)

This is also a widely used index, and in the UK is taken to mean the ratio of a share price to a broadly based market index such as the FT All Share Index. It should not be confused with the Welles Wilder Relative Strength Index, which in this book we have simply called the Welles Wilder Index. In commercial charts, the RSI is superimposed on the lower third of the share price chart, or sometimes in its own box below the main chart.

Because this indicator is a ratio, it will increase as a share moves higher relative to the market, and decrease as a share moves lower relative to the market. As can be seen from examples, its main use for investors is to enable them to focus on shares which are outperforming the market in general, and to avoid those shares which are underperforming the market.

The RSI is easily calculated each day or week by dividing the share price by the index, which can be the All Share Index, or the FTSE100 Index. This is shown in Table 2.2 for BICC between 1st June 1990 and 21st June 1990 using the FTSE100 Index as the divisor.

With the FTSE100 Index around the 3900 mark at the time of writing, values can run from say 0.00025 for penny shares up to about 0.25 for shares which are trading at around the £10 mark. Obviously these cannot be plotted directly on a chart which may have scales running from 10 to 1000. Either the values have to be adjusted by some constant factor, or, more easily, a different scale can be used on the existing chart. Investors are mostly interested in whether the RSI is rising or falling, so actual values of the RSI are of secondary importance to direction as seen on a chart. The scale for the RSI should be such as to restrict the plot of this indicator to the bottom of the chart, but should be wide enough that the movements are not crowded into a very small area. It is difficult to absorb the message from a crowded RSI.

Table 2.2 The Relative Strength Index for BICC versus the FTSE100 Index

Date	Price	FTSE100	Price/FTSE100 ratio
01/06/90	443	2371.4	0.1868
04/06/90	449	2379.0	0.1887
05/06/90	451	2380.1	0.1895
06/06/90	451	2358.5	0.1912
07/06/90	462	2378.4	0.1942
08/06/90	455	2366.6	0.1923
11/06/90	450	2348.8	0.1916
12/06/90	458	2370.7	0.1932
13/06/90	460	2405.4	0.1912
14/06/90	458	2403.0	0.1906
15/06/90	453	2392.3	0.1894
18/06/90	450	2392.3	0.1881
19/06/90	449	2370.5	0.1894
20/06/90	452	2371.2	0.1906
21/06/90	455	2370.3	0.1920

THE WELLES WILDER INDEX

This indicator is among the group called momentum indicators. These indicators are looking at the rate at which a share price is changing; the higher the rate of change the greater the momentum. From this the deduction is that the greater the momentum of the share price, the less likely is it to change direction. The best analogy is with a vehicle moving forward which has to stop before moving in reverse. Initially it has a large momentum which decreases as the brakes are applied. Before moving backwards in reverse it will have a zero momentum, even if this condition holds for only a fraction of a second. As it accelerates away in reverse, the momentum will increase again in the opposite direction. Thus a fall in momentum to zero or almost zero is the signal that the direction is about to change.

The indicator developed by J. Welles Wilder groups prices into rising prices and falling prices. Just as in the case of the span required for a moving average calculation, a period is chosen over which to calculate the indicator. This is usually 14 days, although other periods may be useful in certain circumstances. All the price rises during the first 14-day period are added together to give a quantity which we can call UP. All the price falls during the same period are added to give a quantity which we can call DOWN. The Welles Wilder Index is then given by the following formula:

$$\text{Welles Wilder Index (WWI)} = 100 - \frac{100}{1 + \dfrac{\text{UP}}{\text{DOWN}}}$$

Table 2.3 Calculation of the Welles Wilder Index

Date	Price	Rise	Fall	Total rises in 14 days (UP)	Total falls in 14 days (DOWN)	UP/DOWN	WWI
23/02/96	520						
26/02/96	519		1				
27/02/96	524	5					
28/02/96	525	1					
29/02/96	517		8				
01/03/96	511		6				
04/03/96	514	3					
05/03/96	512		2				
06/03/96	513	1					
07/03/96	512		1				
08/03/96	503		9				
11/03/96	508	5					
12/03/96	509	1					
13/03/96	502		7				
14/03/96	497		5	16	39	0.41	29.08

As an example, the indicator is calculated for the Allied Domecq share price over the same period of time as was used for the moving average calculation. This is shown in Table 2.3. The first entry, for 23rd February 1996, is required only to establish the fall for the next day. The 14-day period then runs from 26th February to 14th March. Each day the price change from the previous day is noted as a rise or a fall. The total of the rises during the 14-day period is then 16p, and the total of the falls is then 39p. The quantity UP/DOWN is 16/39 = 0.41. Thus the WWI value is:

$$\text{WWI} = 100 - \frac{100}{1 + 0.41} = 100 - \frac{100}{1.41} = 29.08$$

The way in which the indicator is calculated means that its value always lies between 0 and 100. This makes it easy to scale onto a share price chart. Another useful aspect of this indicator is that the UP and DOWN parts of the computation have been averaged, and therefore this makes the indicator less liable to react to very short term fluctuations.

The indicator is used by drawing horizontal lines on the chart at the levels corresponding to 70 and 30 (some chartists use 75 and 25). When the indicator moves above 70 it is considered to be overbought, while a fall below 30 means it is considered to be oversold. Although some investors sell as soon as the indicator moves above the 70 mark, and sell as soon as it moves below 30, most chartists wait until the indicator has peaked if it rises above 70, or troughed if it falls below 30. A few chartists adopt the approach of carrying out the appropriate action once the indicator has been above 70 or below 30 for a particular number of days.

Usually the Welles Wilder Index is a leading indicator, i.e. it gives its signal before the share price changes direction, whereas the moving average gives its signal after the price changes direction. Moving averages can therefore be considered to be lagging averages, which act in the confirmatory sense that the change in direction has occurred.

As well as using the indicator in the sense discussed above, where it signals overbought and oversold levels, it also generates chart patterns of the same type as normal price charts, and therefore the same chartist techniques can be applied to the plots of the indicator.

The use of the indicator will be covered in Chapter 11.

3

Trends Within Trends

Share price movement is a complex mixture of trends—very short term, short term, medium term, long term and very long term. In this context a trend is simply a direction of movement. Thus there are uptrends and downtrends and occasionally sideways trends. As a starting point for consideration of the nature of trends, a chart of the Allied Domecq share price over about one month is shown in Figure 3.1, a chart of one year of the price movement is shown in Figure 3.2, while in Figure 3.3 is shown four years of the price movement.

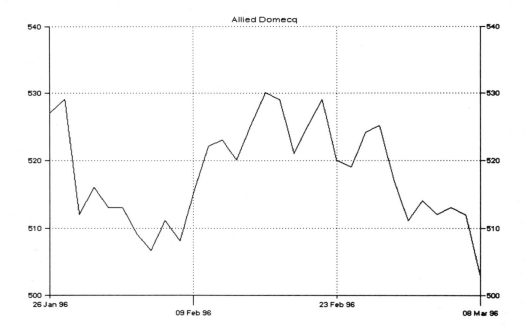

Figure 3.1 About one month of the Allied Domecq share price history

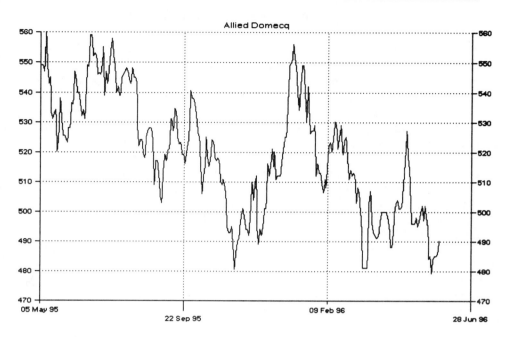

Figure 3.2   About one year of the Allied Domecq share price history

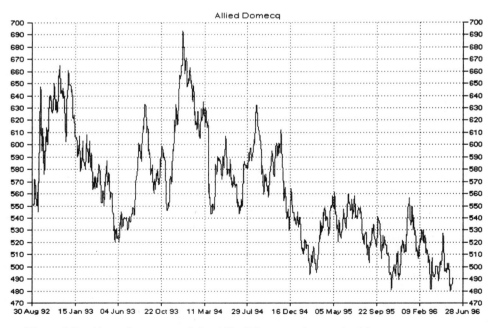

Figure 3.3   About four years of the Allied Domecq share price history

AN EXAMPLE: ALLIED DOMECQ

Taking Figure 3.1 first, it can be seen quite clearly that the share price is moving up and down almost on a daily basis. Underneath this day-to-day variation, it can be seen that after a few days the price has begun a movement which takes it up to its highest point at about the middle of the chart. Thus it can be said that the month's price history shows the existence of an uptrend, which has taken the price from 507p to 530p over the course of six trading days. This uptrend co-exists with the day-to-day up and down movements, which in themselves, if they last for more than one day, can be considered to be mini-uptrends and downtrends. From that halfway point, the price declines again, ending the period at 504p. Thus there is now in existence a downtrend. Both the uptrend and the downtrend appear to have been completed within the time range covered by the chart.

Thus this first chart has shown us the existence of uptrends and downtrends of such a short duration, just a few days, that they are useless from the point of view of investment. It has also shown us the existence of an uptrend which lasts for about 10 days plus a downtrend of similar duration.

This view of just one month's price history gives us no idea of where the price may be headed over the following year. This is because the slice of history is much too short to identify the longer term trends which will take the price onwards for such a length of time. This is put right by the longer, one-year piece of history shown in Figure 3.2. The peak price of 530p attained in Figure 3.1 can now be seen to the right of the middle of the chart for the month of February 1996. Now we can see the existence of more of the short term trends such as those discussed for Figure 3.1, and in addition medium term trends are clearly visible. The peak price of 530p in February 1996 can be seen to be caused by a short term uptrend contained in a longer term downtrend which started at the peak of 555p in December 1995. This point was also the culmination of a medium term uptrend which started from the low of 481p.

Even longer term trends can be seen in Figure 3.3, where a plot of a four-year period of the share price is shown. We can now see more clearly that the medium term downtrend we saw in Figure 3.2 is part of a long term downtrend which started at the end of 1993 when the price reached 692p. This downtrend is still in being at the right-hand side of the chart (May 1996). There are several medium term trends visible which last for over six months, for example the trend which began towards the end of 1992 and continued to June 1993. Still present, of course, in this chart are the short term trends, and the day-to-day random movement which accounts for the fuzziness of the chart. Note the rapid price movement which can be brought about by the short term trends, for example the rise from 548p to 692p in late 1993, and the several sharp falls such as that in late March 1994.

Beside the obvious point that as we open out to more and more of the share price history we can see trends of longer and longer persistence, we should also see that the rises and falls in price which are caused by these trends become large as the length of trend becomes greater.

Thus short term trends in the Allied Domecq share price seem to generate rises and falls of approximately 40p, medium term trends rises and falls of about 120p, and long term trends rises and falls of over 200p. In case these are not immediately obvious, look more closely at the short term trends in 1995, the medium term downtrend in 1993 and the long term trend from the end of 1993 to mid-1996. Many other short term trends and quite a few medium term trends should be visible on closer inspection.

Beside the absolute price range of a trend, another important property is the rate of change of the price for each type of trend. This is obtained by dividing the average price rise or fall by the average length of time for which the trend persists. To carry out such calculations requires several years of history of the share in question. The values will differ considerably from share to share, but as an example, approximate values for Allied Domecq are shown in Table 3.1.

Thus short term trends in the Allied Domecq price show rises of about 2p per day, medium term trends about 0.86p per day and long term trends about 0.33p per day. It is interesting that these rates of change are almost independent of the share price level. Because of that fact, the percentage change per day will vary depending upon where in the share price history the investor is standing when investments are being made. For example, in 1996 a change of 2p per day during the short term trend when the price level was about 500p represented a change of 0.4% per day, a rapid rate of increase in which dealing costs would be rapidly covered even if the investor entered the trend rather late. At the time the price was at the 650p level, the rate of increase was less than 0.3% per day, and such a rate of increase would make it more difficult to recoup dealing costs if the investor entered the short term trend rather late and the trend was of less than average length. Where long term trends have caused a halving or doubling of the share price, the percentage rate of change will obviously be twice the rate at one extreme as at the other.

Investors should always view shares in this light, determining the level of return which might be expected from the various trends, and unless there are grounds which suggest that a short term trend will be very

Table 3.1 Rate of change of the Allied Domecq share price for various trends

Trend	Average length of time	Average price change	Rate of change per day
Short term	20 days	40p	2.00
Medium term	140 days	120p	0.86
Long term	600 days	200p	0.33

profitable, they should concentrate more on medium and long term trends as giving the greatest prospects for success.

The chart patterns which will be discussed in this book are caused by the interaction between trends of various lengths. Thus it will be possible to see short term head and shoulders patterns, for example, which take but a few weeks for completion, the same pattern which may take several months to complete, and very long term versions which may take several years over their formation.

TRENDS TEND TO CONTINUE

This may seem an obvious statement, but it is one of the basic facts upon which chartist techniques are based. A very good analogy can be found with the weather. The Meteorological Office has a record of correctly forecasting the weather about 75% of the time. A number of amateur weather forecasters who look at the behaviour of birds, strings of seaweed, etc., can also achieve similar consistencies. What is not generally realised is that anyone can forecast the weather with at least 70% accuracy. All one has to do is state that tomorrow's weather will be the same as today's. The accuracy comes in because the weather does not swing wildly each day from rain to shine and back again. It stays in trends which usually last for a few days and occasionally for a few weeks. Thus the amateur forecaster will be correct while this condition is maintained, but incorrect on the day the trend changes direction. Try keeping a record yourself for a few weeks and you will see how accurate this method is.

Share prices behave in the same way. Although there is present random day-to-day movement, which will cause the price to rise one day, fall the next, rise the next, fall the next and so on, the trends we discussed above are quite the opposite. They make themselves visible above the random day-to-day movement because of the amount by which they make the price rise or fall. Whereas the random movement might be plus or minus 1p per day, the underlying trend might have a value of plus 1p each day while it lasts. The net result is of course additive, so that the total effect is of a standstill on days when the random movement is downwards, and of a double rise of 2p on days when the random movement is upwards. These are not intended to be exact values, but simply to give an understanding on how the actual price movement observed may have arisen.

Further consideration of trends viewed in the same light as the weather brings one to the conclusion that each day, the most likely event is that the trend, be it short term, medium term or long term, will continue. The least likely event is that it will end. Unfortunately, from the investor's point of view, the most important facts that are required are the beginning and end of a trend, since these allow the investor to enter the market at the lowest price and exit at the higher price. The decision that the uptrend or downtrend will continue is naturally helpful, but is most helpful when an investor is already invested. If he is not invested, then the knowledge that the trend will continue has to be modified by a knowledge of for how long the trend has been in being before a decision to invest can be made. Probably more money has been lost by investors buying in far too late into an uptrend than has been lost by investors incorrectly anticipating the beginning.

Because of the importance of establishing the beginning and end of trends, chartist techniques have tended to focus primarily on this aspect. The features which enable an investor to determine, with various degrees of success, the beginning or end of a trend, be it of a short term, medium term or long term nature, are called reversal patterns. The direction of the trend before the pattern is formed reverses after the pattern has been formed. All of the indicators discussed in this book have been developed as aids to determining that a trend reversal has occurred. Of course, it is also useful to know that a trend should continue, and other patterns which can be used in this sense can be called continuation patterns. In these cases, the direction of the trend once the pattern has been completed is the same as the direction of the trend before the pattern was entered.

DRAWING TRENDLINES

Earlier on, when discussing the lengths of the trends in Figures 3.1, 3.2 and 3.3, their beginnings and ends were more or less guessed at, although the clarity of the trends was such that the guesses were reasonably accurate. A much better idea of the direction of the trends can be obtained if trendlines are drawn.

For uptrends, trendlines are drawn by joining two troughs by a straight line. Since the line is straight, its direction remains constant, and this direction is the direction of the particular trend which is being studied. If the two troughs are a long way apart then the trend is long term. If the two troughs are close together, then the trend can be considered to be short term. Of course a trend which appeared to be a short term trend can turn into a long term trend. When this happens, not only the two original (and close together) troughs lie on the trendline, but subsequent troughs will also fall on the line.

Figure 3.4 shows how a trendline is constructed by joining two such troughs. The figure intentionally gives no indication as to the distance apart in time of the two troughs, and gives no indication as to the vertical distance between them, i.e. the price rise occurring between the two points. Thus the trendline as shown may represent any length of trend from very short term to very long term.

This idea of trendlines can be transferred to a long term chart such as that of the Boots share price (Figure 3.5). A variety of short term, medium term and long term uptrends can be seen.

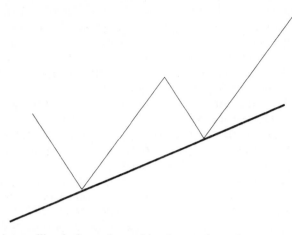

Figure 3.4   A trendline is drawn by making it pass through two successive troughs

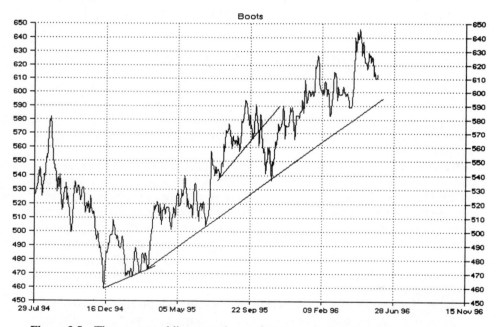

Figure 3.5   Three uptrend lines are shown drawn on the Boots share price

For downtrends, the trendlines are drawn by joining two peaks by a straight line. The same arguments apply as to uptrends, so that short term trends can turn into longer term trends, and third and subsequent peaks may also fall on the trendline. Figure 3.6 shows a downtrend drawn on a chart of the Allied Domecq share price.

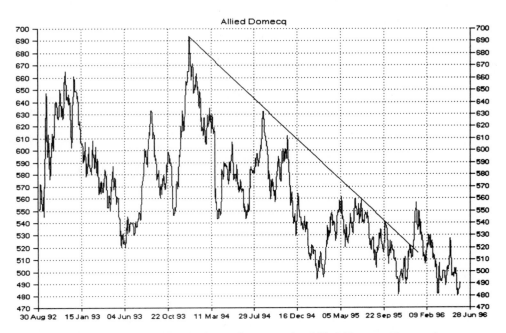

Figure 3.6 A downtrend line is shown drawn on the Allied Domecq share price

HOW TRENDLINES ISOLATE THE TREND

We now come to an important point about trendlines, and that is that a trendline is not the trend itself. As we have seen, a trendline is fairly easy to draw, but we have to be clear that such a trendline simply shows the direction and slope of the trend. The trend itself is certainly not the line drawn by connecting successive peaks or successive troughs, but lies at a position higher than the troughs and lower than the peaks.

This comes about because all trends which are occurring at the same time are additive. It is worth spending some time on this concept because of its importance.

As an example, we can start from the position of having some shorter term trends in existence at the same time as a longer term trend. The short term trends are shown in the upper part of Figure 3.7. There are four successive ones, the first one rising for a few days, the next one falling for a few days, the third one rising again for a few days and the final one being a sideways movement. During the length of time for which these four short term trends are occurring, we can see what the effect will be of having a longer term trend present which is maintained for the whole time period in question. This trend can be an uptrend or a downtrend, and for this

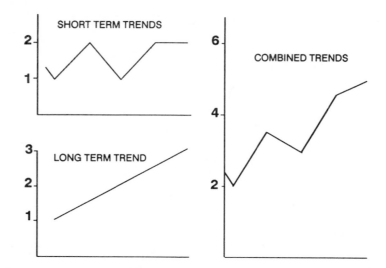

Figure 3.7 Short term trends can be combined additively with a long term trend to give the final result shown on the right

example is taken to be an uptrend. This longer term uptrend is shown in the lower left of Figure 3.7. Since the effect of all trends which are present at any one time is additive, the actual price movement that we see is obtained by adding these shorter term and longer term trends together. You can easily do this for yourself since numerical values have been put on the left-hand scale in the figure. The net result is shown in the right-hand part of Figure 3.7.

If we now draw a trendline on this net result using the same procedure as for the Boots and Allied Domecq charts, as has been done in Figure 3.8, we can see that the drawn trendline has exactly the same upward slope as the original longer term trend we started from in Figure 3.7. In other words, this simple method of drawing a trendline has isolated the direction and duration of the longer term trend for us. Note the important fact that the numerical values that we read off from the vertical scale for the trendline are not the same as those for the original trend. Thus our original contention that the trendline is not quite the same thing as the trend itself is justified.

Exactly the same approach can be used to isolate downtrends from combinations of shorter and longer term downtrends, and even to isolate uptrends from combinations of short term downtrends and longer term uptrends, and downtrends from combinations of short term uptrends and longer term downtrends.

Since the most important features of a trend are its direction and its time of persistence, the fact that both of these pieces of information are so

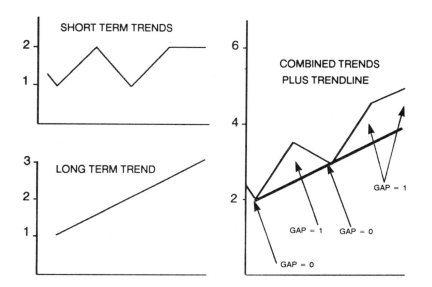

Figure 3.8 A trendline (heavy line) is now drawn on the combined trends from Figure 3.7. This has exactly the same slope as the original long term trend, thus the trendline has isolated the long term trend. Note that the short term trends can be recovered by plotting the gaps between the actual data and the superimposed trendline

easily obtained by drawing a trendline outweighs the fact that, numerically, trends and trendlines are somewhat different.

The more mathematically minded reader who has been trying the exercise of adding trends together where the successive short term trends are not of equal magnitude and timescale will find that the trendline drawn from such a starting point will not have the same direction and slope as the original longer term trend. Thus implicit in the drawing of trendlines is that the trends of shorter duration than the trend represented by the trendline being drawn are symmetrical, i.e. their upward-moving legs last for exactly the same duration as their downward-moving legs, and the movement covers the same price range. If trends are considered to be cyclical in nature, then both of these requirements fall into place, since any particular trend will rise for exactly the same length of time that it will fall, the sequence being repeated until the trend terminates. The advantage of viewing trends as being cyclical in nature is fundamental to the technique of channel analysis, which is discussed in Chapter 13.

So far we have been drawing trendlines as straight lines on the chart, looking for troughs or peaks which fall on such lines. Since we have just observed that trends are cyclical in nature, then any trendlines which are straight lines represent trends whose cycles occur over very long time scales. Any trends whose cycles repeat at much smaller intervals will not be straight lines but curves. Thus it is perfectly proper to draw curving

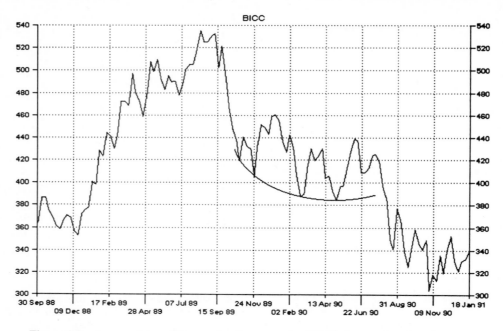

Figure 3.9 A curved trendline can be drawn on the BICC share price chart from the latter half of 1989 to the middle of 1990

trendlines as well as straight ones. As an example of this, a curved trendline is drawn on the BICC price chart shown in Figure 3.9.

The curved line in Figure 3.9 begins as a downtrend line. There is of course a difficulty with curved trendlines if we take the analogy with straight trendlines too far. This difficulty arises at the point where a curved downtrend becomes horizontal before rising again. We have distinguished straight uptrend lines from downtrend lines by virtue of the fact that the downtrend line connects peaks while uptrend lines connect troughs. Where a curved downtrend becomes horizontal before rising as an uptrend, logic would dictate that we discontinue the curved downtrend line joining peaks and continue a new line with the same rate of curvature which now joins the troughs. This is a case where we should ignore logic, since it makes much more sense to continue the same downtrend line onwards as an uptrend line, provided we still have new peaks falling on this line. Taking this logic further, it is equally sensible to draw a curved downtrend line where troughs are connected and continue this type of line onwards as an uptrend line.

This approach shows that the drawing of straight trendlines is not following logic but is simply following a convention whereby downtrends connect peaks and uptrends connect troughs. We shall not rock the boat but will continue to use this same convention for straight lines while adopting the more flexible method of dealing with curved trends.

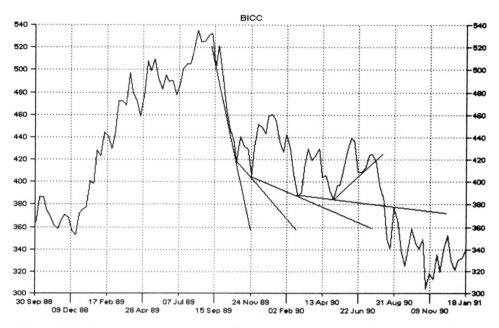

Figure 3.10 The curved trend shown in Figure 3.9 can also be highlighted by drawing a series of straight trendlines. These are called fanlines for obvious reasons

DISPLAYING CURVED TRENDS AS A SERIES OF STRAIGHT LINES

Many chartists avoid wherever possible the drawing of curved lines, and use a different approach to the highlighting of curved trends which uses the concept of fanlines. This is shown in Figure 3.10 for the BICC share price. An uptrend line is drawn from a major low point to the next trough. When a subsequent trough is formed, a second trendline is drawn from the same starting point as the first trendline to this new trough. With each succeeding trough which fails to fall on the initial trendline, a new trendline is drawn, but starting from the same initial point. Eventually the trendlines form an obvious fan shape emanating from this starting point.

What these fan lines are doing is showing that the underlying long term downtrend is flattening out, eventually to turn over and become an up-trend. In this particular case the change from a downtrend to an uptrend was short lived, and the share resumed its downward path.

4

Theoretical Chart Patterns

Chart patterns are an essential part of technical analysis, but too many practitioners use them slavishly without real understanding. Chart patterns are successful in predicting the future direction of the market or of a share price, but are also frequently unsuccessful. Part of the failure can be attributed to an eagerness on the part of the investor which has him believing a particular pattern is being formed without waiting for further confirmation. Part of the failure can also be attributed to a failure of the pattern itself. It is this author's view that an understanding of the reasons why patterns are formed and why patterns sometimes fail is essential if an investor is to maximise the returns from investment in shares. This understanding will also lead to a more patient approach. Nothing but consistent losses can follow an investor who is continually jumping the gun and entering the market before the change in direction of a trend is confirmed. An investor who grasps the fundamental processes which lead to the formation of chart patterns will allow the market itself to dictate the correct timing for an investment decision. Such an investor will inevitably come out ahead of his less patient colleague.

In later chapters in this book, chart patterns are put into two categories, those which we can call reversal patterns and those which we can call continuation patterns. A reversal pattern is one where the direction of the trend at the point where it leaves the pattern is the reverse of the direction of the trend when it enters the pattern. Thus an uptrend becomes converted into a downtrend, or a downtrend becomes converted into an uptrend. A continuation pattern is one where the direction of the trend when it leaves the pattern is the same as the direction of the trend when it enters the pattern. Thus an uptrend passes through the pattern and still remains as an uptrend, and similarly for a downtrend.

CYCLICAL MOVEMENT

All of the patterns which will be discussed can take place on a small, medium or large scale, i.e. can complete the formation in a matter of days,

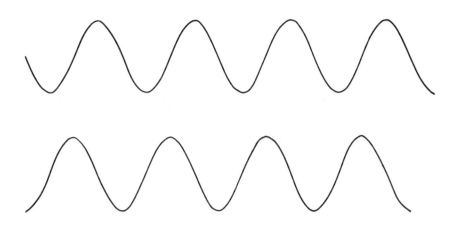

Figure 4.1 These two sine waves have identical amplitude (trough to peak vertical distances) and identical wavelengths (peak to peak horizontal distances). Because their peaks do not occur at exactly the same points in time their phases are different

weeks or years. This is more easily understandable when it is considered that the patterns are formed from various combinations of cyclical movements in the market. Before taking this question of cycles any further it is necessary to have a clear idea of what is meant by a cyclical price movement. Such a movement is shown in Figure 4.1. The shape of this repetitive movement is probably better recognised by using the term 'sine wave'. Any sine wave is completely defined by three quantities: the wavelength, the amplitude and the phase. For the purposes of this book, it is not necessary to delve into any mathematics, but simply to define what is meant by these three quantities defining the sine wave. By doing this we also define the cycles which are occurring in share price movement.

The wavelength of the sine wave is simply the distance from one point in the wave to the next similar point, i.e. the distance between two successive peaks, or the distance between two successive troughs. For share prices this wavelength will be in days for very short wavelength cycles, in weeks for medium wavelength cycles and in years for long wavelength cycles. The amplitude of the sine wave is the vertical distance moved, i.e. the vertical distance between a trough and the next or previous peak. This will be measured in points for an index such as the FTSE100, and in pence or pounds for a share price. The third quantity that specifies a sine wave is the phase. This simply means the distance between some arbitrary starting point and the first trough or peak in the wave. Thus the two sine waves shown in Figure 4.1 look identical, and are identical as far as amplitude and wavelength are concerned. They have different phases because the peaks in the upper sine wave occur at a different point in time from those in the lower sine wave. By shifting the phase in the lower sine wave, i.e. moving the whole sine wave to the right, a position can be reached in which the two waves can be exactly superimposed. When this happens the two waves are identical in every respect—wavelength, amplitude and phase. As far as the stock market is concerned, we shall not apply exact values to the phase of a sine wave. It is sufficient to recognise when two waves are exactly in phase at some particular time of interest (two peaks coincide), when they are exactly out of phase at some particular time (a peak of one coincides with a trough of the other) and when they are partly out of phase (neither two peaks nor a peak and a trough coincide). Patterns in share price movement will become much more meaningful with these fairly simple concepts of phase. Note the important property of sine waves in that they are perfectly symmetrical. For this reason patterns which are composed of only one cycle or perhaps a combination of two cycles are usually symmetrical about a vertical centre line. Where three cycles are involved the patterns may or may not be symmetrical about a vertical centre line.

The proper meaning of the term 'cycle' as applied to a sine wave is the part of the wave from any starting point on the wave to the next similar point, e.g. from one trough to the next, from one peak to the next or from a point halfway up a left-hand rising side to the next point halfway up a left-hand rising side. This is one cycle of the sine wave. However, in technical analysis, the term has become misused to apply to the whole sine wave. Thus the term '20-day cycle' means a sine wave with a wavelength of 20 days, but of unspecified amplitude (and phase).

At this point, it is useful to clarify the trends which were discussed in the last chapter in terms of sine waves or cycles. An uptrend is the part of the cyclical movement from a trough to the succeeding peak, while a downtrend is the part of the cyclical movement from a peak to the next trough. Thus an uptrend is one half of a complete cycle using the correct meaning of the term 'cycle' and a downtrend is also one half of a complete cycle. It should now be obvious that the length of an uptrend or a downtrend is one half of the wavelength of the cyclical movement concerned. Thus cycles of wavelength 20 days from peak to peak will give uptrends of 10 days and downtrends of 10 days.

Before moving on to the way in which various patterns are produced by combinations of cycles, it is necessary to point out that in all of these theoretical shapes, cycles of much shorter wavelength than the timescale of the pattern itself as well as day-to-day random price movements are omitted for the purposes of clarity. Naturally in the real world of the charts that will be analysed throughout this book, these other movements all co-exist, but since they have no effect on the underlying longer term patterns being observed they can be ignored for the purposes of analysis.

TREND REVERSAL PATTERNS

Single Top

Rounded top This is the simplest possible pattern, since, as mentioned above, if cycles of very much shorter wavelength and random movements are ignored, all that is left is a curved trend which is the top part of a cyclical waveform of the appropriate wavelength. Only one such cyclical waveform is involved, and there is no interaction with any other waveform of say half, one-quarter or one-eighth of the dominant waveform. The derivation of a rounded top formation from one waveform is shown in Figure 4.2. The rounded top pattern should be symmetrical for a limited distance either side of a vertical line drawn through the peak price, and this line of symmetry is shown in Figure 4.2. The cleaner the rounded top, i.e. the freer from combination with other cyclical movements, the further does the symmetry extend either side of the line of symmetry. Rounded tops can take perhaps a year for their complete formation or may only take a few weeks, depending upon the nature of the dominant cycle causing the formation.

Sharp top The rounded top reflects the fact that sentiment about the share price is taking a long time to unravel, so that there is a long battle between the buyers and the sellers. On the other hand a sharp top reflects a rapid change in sentiment for the worse. In cyclic terms, there is a short term cycle superimposed on a longer term cycle such that the two peaks are more or less coincident in time. The way in which a sharp top is formed is shown in Figure 4.3.

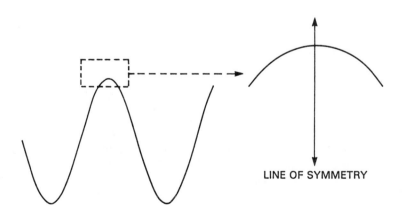

LINE OF SYMMETRY

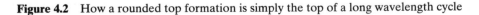

Figure 4.2 How a rounded top formation is simply the top of a long wavelength cycle

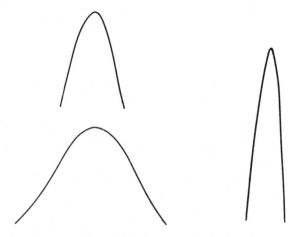

Figure 4.3 How a sharp top formation (on the right) is simply the coincidence of the peaks of two different cycles (on the left). This coincidence accentuates the rate of rise and fall

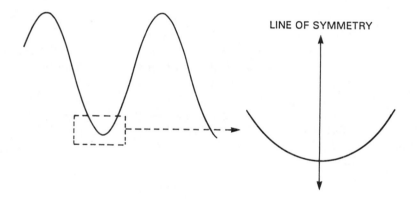

LINE OF SYMMETRY

Figure 4.4 How a rounded bottom formation is simply the bottom of a long wavelength cycle

Single Bottom

Rounded bottom   All of the comments about a rounded top apply to a rounded bottom, with the exception that a rounded bottom is the bottom part of a cyclical waveform. An example of a rounded bottom with a line of symmetry is shown in Figure 4.4.

Sharp bottom   This is formed in the same way as the sharp top, with a short term cycle superimposed on a longer term cycle. The troughs in both

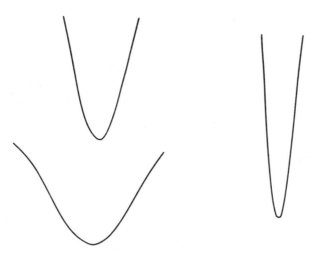

Figure 4.5 How a sharp bottom formation (on the right) is simply the coincidence of the troughs of two different cycles (on the left). This coincidence accentuates the rate of fall and rise

occur more or less at the same point in time. An example of a sharp bottom is shown in Figure 4.5.

Double Top

Now we move on to a pattern which is caused by the combination of two cycles. The dominant cycle is the one which causes the pattern to be a reversal pattern, i.e. the dominant cycle is passing through its peak. In the absence of another cycle we would simply have a rounded top formation.

In addition to the dominant cycle we have another one present which is reaching its trough as the dominant cycle reaches its peak. This second cycle usually has a wavelength of about half that of the dominant cycle. Thus while the dominant cycle is passing through its maximum there is time for two complete waveforms of the second cycle to be formed. The way a double top is formed from these two cycles is shown in Figure 4.6 along with the line of symmetry.

The double top formation will start to lose its symmetry if the trough of the second cycle is not exactly coincident.

Double Bottom

All of the comments about a double top apply equally well to a double bottom, with the exception that the dominant cycle is passing through its trough while the second cycle is passing through its peak. The wavelength

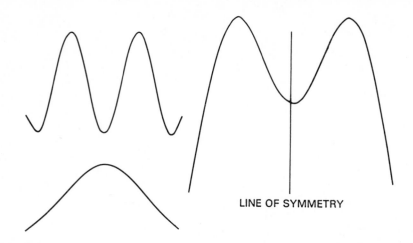

LINE OF SYMMETRY

Figure 4.6 How a double top pattern is formed by the coincidence of the trough of one cycle with the peak of a longer term cycle

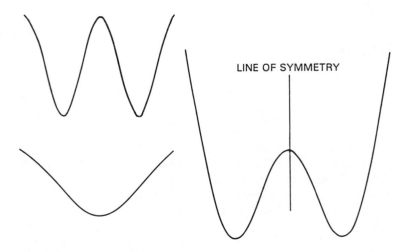

LINE OF SYMMETRY

Figure 4.7 How a double bottom pattern is formed by the coincidence of the peak of one cycle with the trough of a longer term cycle

of the second cycle is usually about half that of the dominant cycle. A symmetrical double bottom formation is shown in Figure 4.7.

Triple Top

A triple top is formed by the combination of two cycles, the second cycle being much more different in wavelength from the dominant cycle than is the case with double tops. This means that while the dominant cycle is passing through its maximum there is time for three complete waveforms of the second cycle to be formed. A completely symmetrical triple top is shown in Figure 4.8. Because there are two ways in which the formation can be asymmetric, a completely symmetric triple top formation is not as common as the asymmetric versions. The asymmetry can take the form of a different distance between the first and second tops compared with the second and third tops, or of different heights for each of the three tops or different levels for the two troughs between the three tops. Such asymmetric triple tops are shown in Figure 4.9.

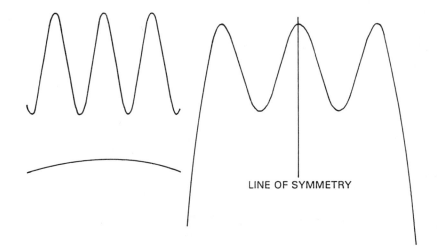

LINE OF SYMMETRY

Figure 4.8 Triple tops are formed by the same process as double tops, but the subordinate cycle (upper) is of much shorter wavelength than the dominant cycle (lower)

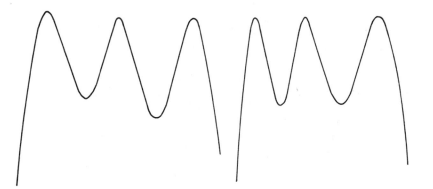

Figure 4.9 Asymmetric triple tops. The left-hand peaks and troughs are not at the same levels. The right-hand peaks are unevenly spaced in time

Triple Bottom

As with the relationship between the previous top and bottom formations the same comments about symmetry and asymmetry apply to triple bottoms. Triple bottoms are caused by the dominant cycle passing through its minimum while interacting with a second cycle of considerably shorter wavelength. Examples of symmetric and asymmetric triple bottoms are shown in Figures 4.10 and 4.11.

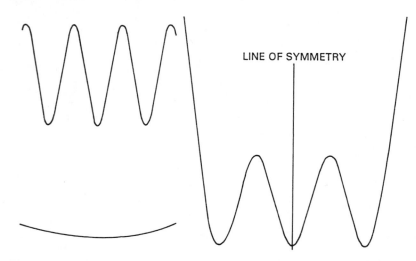

Figure 4.10   Triple bottoms are formed by the same process as double bottoms, but the subordinate cycle (upper) is of much shorter wavelength than the dominant cycle (lower)

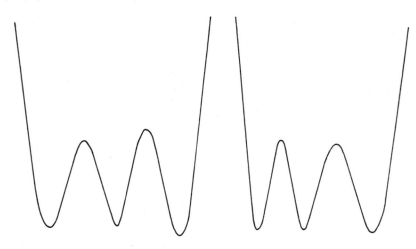

Figure 4.11   Asymmetric triple bottoms. The left-hand peaks and troughs are not at the same levels. The right-hand peaks are unevenly spaced in time

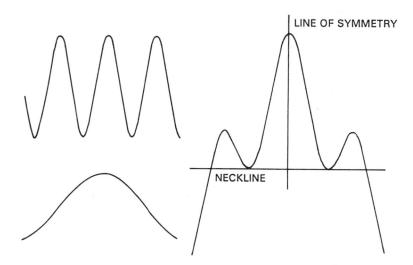

Figure 4.12 A head and shoulders is formed by a combination of a long term cycle and a short time cycle. The head is higher than the shoulders because a short term peak coincides with the maximum of the long term peak

Head and Shoulders

Head and shoulders formations result from a similar combination of cycles to a triple top. The amplitude of the secondary cycle is at its maximum at the point where the middle of the three cycles occurs, and therefore causes the middle peak to be higher than either of the outside peaks. The middle peak is therefore the 'head' and the outside peaks the 'shoulders' of the pattern. The 'neckline' of the pattern is the horizontal line which joins the two troughs, one either side of the head. An example of a symmetrical head and shoulders pattern is shown in Figure 4.12. The line of symmetry is the vertical passing through the centre of the head.

More often than not, the pattern is not quite symmetrical. The usual asymmetry is that the neckline is not quite horizontal, but slopes either upward or downward. Occasionally the neckline is horizontal but one shoulder is higher than the other. Rarer examples of asymmetry show a double head or a double shoulder.

Inverted Head and Shoulders

Inverted head and shoulders are formed by a similar combination of cycles to a triple bottom, but the middle bottom falls to a lower level than the bottom on either side. Since the pattern is inverted, it is still in order to refer to the neckline and shoulders. The shoulders of an inverted head and shoulders are of course the low points reached by the bottoms at each side

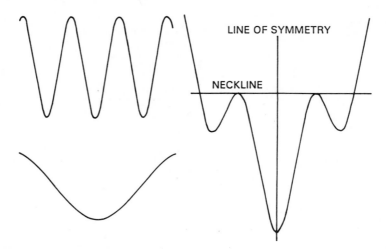

Figure 4.13   An inverted head and shoulders is formed by a combination of a long term cycle and a short term cycle. The inverted head is lower than the shoulders because a short term trough coincides with the minimum of the long term trough

of the centre one, while the neckline is the line joining the peaks which lie between the inverted head and the inverted shoulders. A perfectly symmetrical inverted head and shoulders pattern is shown in Figure 4.13.

TREND CONTINUATION PATTERNS

The reversal patterns discussed above are reversal patterns simply because of the status of the dominant cycle, which is either topping out or bottoming out. On the other hand the trend continuation patterns are ones in which the dominant cycle is not at a top or bottom but is either rising towards the peak or falling towards the trough, but still with some way to go.

Uptrend

An uptrend is a combination of a dominant cycle in a rising mode with a cycle of shorter wavelength superimposed. The troughs of the uptrend fall either on a straight line if the dominant cycle has a particularly long wavelength, or on a curve if the dominant cycle has a more obvious curve. If the curve is of increasing slope then the dominant trend has some way to go to its peak, whereas with a decreasing slope the dominant trend is approaching its peak. An example of a straight line uptrend is shown in Figure 4.14.

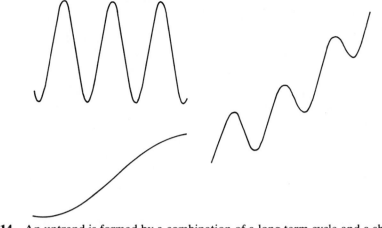

Figure 4.14 An uptrend is formed by a combination of a long term cycle and a short term cycle. The dominant longer term cycle is on its way up to its maximum

Downtrend

Again, a downtrend is a combination of a dominant cycle which is in a falling mode with a cycle of shorter wavelength superimposed. The peaks of the downtrend can fall on a straight line if the dominant cycle is of particularly long wavelength, or on a curve if the dominant cycle is not of particularly long wavelength. If the down slope is increasing in curvature then the downtrend has some way to go, whereas if the down slope is decreasing in curvature the downtrend is approaching its trough. An example of a straight downtrend is shown in Figure 4.15.

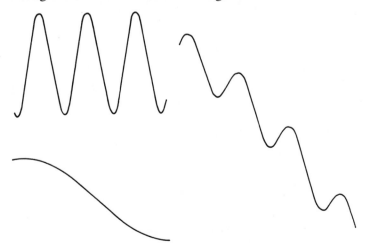

Figure 4.15 A downtrend is formed by a combination of a long term cycle and a short term cycle. The dominant longer term cycle is on its way down to its minimum

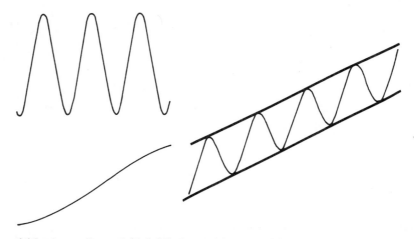

Figure 4.16   An upchannel (right) is formed by a combination of a very long term cycle (lower left) and a short term cycle (upper left). The dominant longer term cycle is on its way up to its maximum. Because of its long wavelength, the upward leg is almost a straight line

Upchannels

Upchannels are a particular form of uptrend. In this case the secondary cycles are of such regularity that lines joining the troughs and lines joining the peaks can be drawn parallel to each other in the case of straight channels or concentric in the case of curved channels. The same comments about straight and curved uptrends apply to upchannels. An example of a straight upchannel is shown in Figure 4.16.

Downchannels

Downchannels are a specific form of downtrend again with the secondary cycles of such regular amplitude that the lines joining the peaks and troughs are parallel in the case of straight channels and concentric in the case of curved channels. The same comments about straight and curved downtrends apply to downchannels. An example of a straight downchannel is shown in Figure 4.17.

AMBIGUOUS PATTERNS

The trend reversal and trend continuation patterns were so called because more often than not they correctly call the future direction of the trend. Therefore as the particular pattern is unfolding, the investor has a reasonable expectation for the future course of events. Ambiguous patterns are

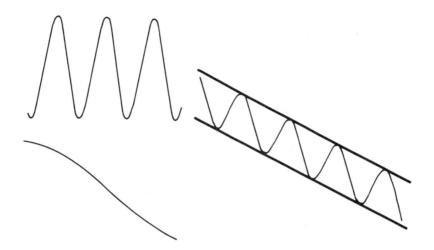

Figure 4.17 A downchannel (right) is formed by a combination of a very long term cycle (lower left) and a short term cycle (upper left). The dominant longer term cycle is on its way down to its minimum. Because of its long wavelength, the downward leg is almost a straight line

in a different category, since they sometimes act as continuation patterns and sometimes as reversal patterns. Although in the next chapter we urge caution on the part of the investor, who should wait for confirmation of a pattern formation, it is doubly important that an investor should wait for the following ambiguous patterns to be resolved before making any investment decision.

Support Lines

In a sense, a support line is similar to a perfect triple bottom. It is formed by the combination of a long wavelength cycle that is passing through a horizontal phase and a cycle of much shorter wavelength. This cycle is of much shorter wavelength relative to the dominant cycle than is the case with the triple bottom.

In the case of support lines, the price falls to a level before bouncing back upwards, and this level is one that has seen similar behaviour previously. A support level can be revisited by the share price at very long time intervals. A horizontal line can be drawn at this support level. Buyers are attracted as the support level is reached, thus causing the price to rise. Often the support level is at a 'round' level such as a multiple of 100p. Once a support level has been breached by a fall in price below it, the level then often becomes a resistance level. An example of a support line is shown in Figure 4.18.

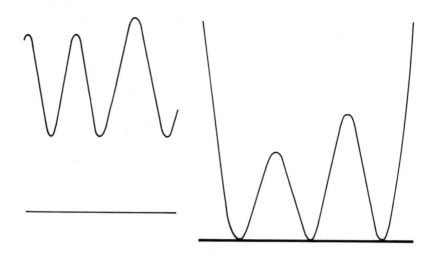

Figure 4.18 Support lines are formed by a similar process as triple bottoms, but the subordinate cycle (upper) is of much shorter wavelength than the dominant cycle (lower) and may be of irregular amplitude. The dominant cycle is horizontal

Resistance Lines

A resistance line is formed similarly to a support line by a combination of a long term cycle passing through its horizontal phase plus a cycle of shorter wavelength. When the price rises to this level, it then rebounds downwards. The level is one which has seen similar behaviour in the past and, as with support lines, may be revisited at quite widely separated time intervals. Again, such levels frequently occur at rounded price levels such as multiples of 10p or 100p. An example is shown in Figure 4.19. Once breached by a rise in price above the resistance level, such resistance lines can often become future support lines.

Rectangles

A rectangle is a specific form of channel which, rather than rising or falling as an upchannel or downchannel, is moving horizontally. It is therefore formed by a combination of a long term cycle which is moving horizontally, plus an extremely regular short term cycle with constant amplitude. It is a congested area which is bounded on the upper side by a resistance line and on the lower side by a support line. The price therefore oscillates between these two levels. Obviously there comes a time when the price breaks out on either the upper or lower side, but which of these two will occur is not predictable. An example of a rectangle is shown in Figure 4.20.

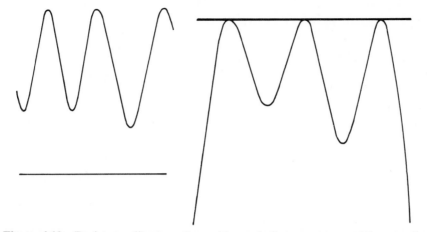

Figure 4.19 Resistance lines are formed by a similar process as triple tops, but the subordinate cycle (upper) is of much shorter wavelength than the dominant cycle (lower) and may be of irregular amplitude. The dominant cycle is at a horizontal phase

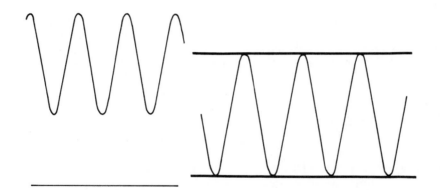

Figure 4.20 Rectangles are formed by a similar process to upchannels and downchannels, but the dominant cycle is passing through a horizontal phase

Triangles

Triangles can take two main forms. The first is where the price movement is becoming more pronounced as time unfolds. These are called expanding triangles, which are fairly rare in occurrence. The other form is where the price movement is decreasing as time unfolds, so that the triangle is contracting. These are much more common, and fall into various categories such as ascending right-angled, descending right-angled, isosceles (two sides equal in length) and scalene (all sides unequal in length). The latter is also called a wedge.

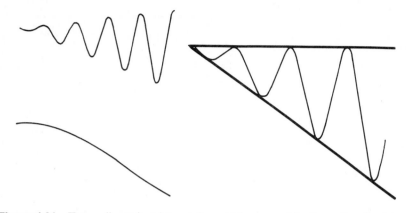

Figure 4.21 Expanding triangles are formed by a combination of a short term cycle with an increasing amplitude and a long term cycle that may be rising, or, as above, falling or passing through a horizontal phase

Expanding triangle　Whereas the head and shoulders and inverted head and shoulders patterns were characterised by the central of three complete waveforms of the secondary cycles being of greater amplitude than the outside ones, the expanding triangle has the secondary cycles increasing in amplitude as the price unfolds. At some point the price has to break out, either on the upside or on the downside. An example of an expanding triangle is shown in Figure 4.21.

Ascending triangle　This formation is a right-angled triangle with the upper side horizontal. It is caused by the combination of a dominant cycle which is in a rising phase and a shorter wavelength cycle whose amplitude is decreasing with time. Thus the usual resolution of the triangle is that the rise will continue, since the dominant cycle is in a rising mode. However, as with all contracting triangle formations, if the price exits through the apex the significance is lost. An example is shown in Figure 4.22.

Descending triangle　This formation is caused by the same combination of cycles as in the ascending triangle, the difference being that the dominant cycle is in a falling phase. It is this direction of the dominant cycle that leads to the usual resolution of the pattern into a continuing fall. The usual resolution of the triangle does not follow if the price exits through the apex. An example is shown in Figure 4.23.

Isosceles triangle　This formation is caused by the same combination of cycles as the right-angled triangles, but with the important difference that

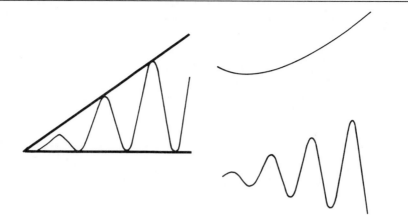

Figure 4.22 Ascending triangles are formed by a combination of a short term cycle with a decreasing amplitude and a long term cycle that is rising

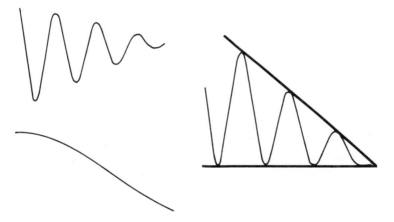

Figure 4.23 Descending triangles are formed by a combination of a short term cycle with a decreasing amplitude and a long term cycle that is falling

the dominant cycle is passing through a horizontal phase, neither rising nor falling. Thus the triangle is essentially symmetrical about a horizontal line through its apex. Whether the triangle is a reversal or continuation pattern depends upon the status of an even longer term cycle than the triangle dominant cycle, but the balance seems to lie slightly on the side of continuation. An exit through the apex takes the meaning out of the triangle. An example is shown in Figure 4.24.

Scalene triangle or wedge　It is possible to have triangles which are wedge shaped, i.e. which are neither right-angled nor symmetrical in the sense

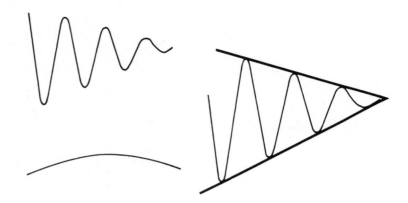

Figure 4.24 Isosceles triangles are formed by a combination of a short term cycle with a decreasing amplitude and a long term cycle that is almost horizontal

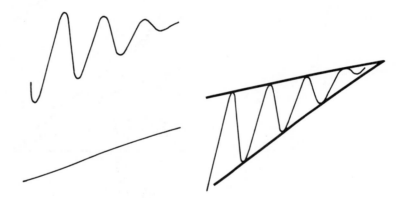

Figure 4.25 Wedges are formed by a combination of a descending or ascending triangle and a long term cycle that is falling or rising

that the isosceles triangle is. The usual resolution of a wedge is that the price reverses the direction of its trend. An example of a wedge is shown in Figure 4.25.

Flags

Flags are specific varieties of triangles, and occasionally channels, which persist for only a short period of time. In general chartists take this period to be a maximum of three weeks. The flag is halfway up or down a steep trend, and as such represents a breathing point before the trend continues

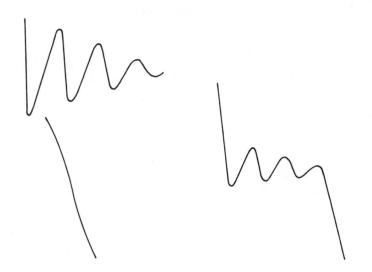

Figure 4.26 Flags are formed by a combination of a very short term cycle of reducing amplitude and a rapidly rising or falling medium term cycle

in its previous direction. All the various types of triangles noted above are possible as these mini-versions, and for channels the slope for the short duration in which they persist can be upward or downward sloping. Examples of flags are shown in Figure 4.26.

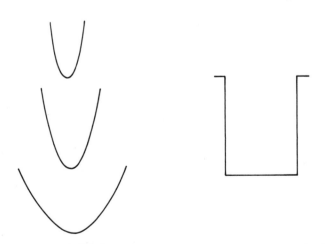

Figure 4.27 An earthquake is formed by a combination of cycles that are all falling to a trough simultaneously

Earthquakes

An earthquake is a fairly rare pattern which appears to be ignored in other texts on technical analysis or charting techniques. In a real-life earthquake a portion of land can slip down below the level of the surrounding land, the edges of the fall being vertical. A similar occurrence can occur in share prices, from the point of view that a sudden vertical fall in price can be matched later by an equally vertical rise. When the vertical rise will occur is not predictable, and the rapidity of the rise is such that it is difficult for the investor to climb aboard the rise at a sensible price level. The interesting facet of the earthquake pattern that can be of great use to investors is that it seems to be an aberration in the longer term trend of the share price, in other words the price seems to continue after the vertical rise with the same trend that it had before the vertical fall. An example is shown in Figure 4.27.

5

Confirmation of Patterns

The buying and selling of shares based purely on pattern formation is but one part of the overall concept of technical analysis. With practice it is possible to realise good returns from investment decisions based purely on the patterns which we discussed in the last chapter, and the next few chapters will concentrate on this aspect. Later chapters discuss the importance of indicators as aids to buying and selling decisions, and there is no doubt that the investor who uses all the tools at his disposal, pattern formation and indicators, will achieve more consistent results than the one who relies solely on patterns. That being said, it is still necessary to show how investment decisions can be based on pattern formation.

All successful investors knowingly or unknowingly use methods which are based on taking advantage of probability. Taking a very simplified view, investors who do not do this will have only a 50% chance of being correct in an investment decision. If dealing costs and the difference, i.e. spread, of buying and selling prices for a share are taken into consideration then the odds move against the investor, perhaps as far as giving him only a 40% chance of success. The rationale behind using pattern formation for investment is that share prices passing through a recognised reversal pattern, such as those discussed in the last chapter, more often than not will show a change in the direction of the trend. Share prices passing through a continuation pattern will more often than not show a continuation in the direction of the trend. Where investors often go wrong is in translating the phrase 'more often than not' into a very high probability, such as 90% or more, that the future course of the share price will continue as predicted. The probability is nothing like as high as that, and at a guess a value of 55% is nearer to the mark. This may not sound high enough to make profits, but over a large number of transactions the investor will inevitably make profits. Better profits will be made if the investor employs a good stop loss method, so that losing situations are terminated quickly, while winning situations are allowed to run. A good analogy for the value of small favourable percentages is with roulette, where the percentage in favour of the house due to the presence of a zero or double zero is quite small, but few people would question the statement that casinos make profits.

The investor should pay much more attention to reversal patterns than continuation patterns for the simple reason that recognition that a share is passing through a continuation pattern usually requires no further action from the investor. On the other hand a reversal formation can signal to the investor that a buying opportunity is becoming imminent. As we discuss later in this chapter, an investor should never be in the position that he relies on a topping pattern to tell him when to sell. For this reason this chapter discusses reversal patterns at bottoms, and at what stage in their development that a buying decision can be made with the greatest chance of success. For the investor in shares, reversal patterns at tops are considered more in the light of an indication to the investor that the share should be put on the back burner for a while. Investors in options fall into a totally different category, since the knowledge that a share may be in a falling trend is just as valuable as the knowledge that a share may now be in a rising trend.

In order to achieve the small favourable percentage which is available from correct recognition of a pattern, it is vital to wait for confirmation that a pattern is complete. It is only then that the investor can move the balance of probability in his favour. The necessity of doing this is readily illustrated by an example of a falling share price which has apparently bottomed out, as shown in Figure 5.1. The investor would therefore be contemplating buying the share in question.

The first thought is that this is a rounded bottom formation, since the shape traced by the price movement so far has passed through a fairly gentle minimum. More thought will lead to the conclusion that the pattern

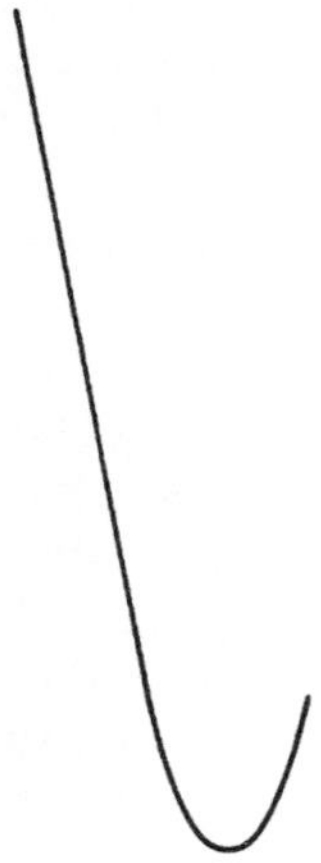

Figure 5.1   A falling share price which appears to have bottomed out

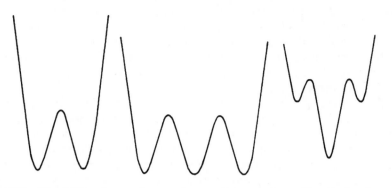

Figure 5.2 The falling share price may be entering a variety of bottoming formations

so far could also be the start of a double bottom, a triple bottom or even an inverted head and shoulders where the first trough is somewhat more rounded than usual. These possibilities are shown in Figure 5.2. If this is the case, not too much damage is done by buying at this early stage in the pattern formation, since these other possibilities are all trend reversal patterns, and therefore there is no advantage in continuing to hold off from the share for any length of time.

This approach neglects some other possibilities, such as a downtrend or downchannel formation, as shown in Figure 5.3. It would be incorrect to buy at this juncture since these patterns are trend continuation patterns. Such premature buying would expose the investor to a loss, and it could well be years before the share price moves back above this original buying level.

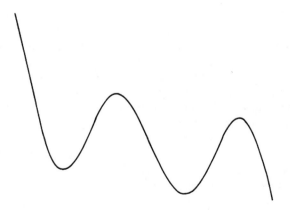

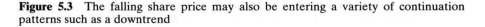

Figure 5.3 The falling share price may also be entering a variety of continuation patterns such as a downtrend

The above comments lead to the conclusion that we need a set of rules to apply to enable us to know whether a pattern has been completed, i.e. the formation in Figure 5.1 does turn out to be a rounded bottom, or whether it is incomplete, i.e. the formation in Figure 5.1 is the first part of a new downtrend. The rules should be concerned with deciding how far up from the bottom of the first part of the formation shown in Figure 5.1 we should allow the share price to rise before buying. This can only be done by studying a large number of shares in order to decide how far shares rise from the bottom before the next downward wave in a downtrend commences. Once a rise exceeds this usual value, then we can say with much more confidence that the downtrend is not going to occur, and that we are embarked on an uptrend, and therefore it is correct to buy. If the price turns down before rising this distance, then we can wait for the next phase of the pattern to unfold before taking a decision. When we come to the chapters on indicators, it will be seen that most of the rules are already enshrined in the way in which indicators are calculated and used, which enforces the view expressed earlier that the best results are obtained from a combination of pattern formation and indicator techniques.

Of the possible bottoming patterns of single bottom, double bottom, triple bottom and inverted head and shoulders, the single bottom, be it of the rounded or sharp variety, is the most difficult to establish. The reason is that all of the other patterns give an intermediate rise followed by a fall before a further rise, and the level reached by the first rise can be used to designate a ceiling through which the price must rise before the share can be considered a buy. Another way of looking at things is that the level of the first rise is a resistance level, so that a rise through it is a good positive sign. The single rounded bottom has no such level, and therefore there is nothing to indicate that the share has passed into a bullish phase. Fortunately the single bottom is the least common of the bottoming formations. Because of this fact, and the difficulty associated with it of determining when its formation is complete, investors should not take action on a single bottom formation unless one or more indicators can confirm that the new trend of the share price is upwards. Never forget the golden rule that amongst the large number of shares which can be followed, there will nearly always be another share in which a more significant pattern can be found. If this is not the case, then do nothing until such an opportunity does arise. Never force an investment decision out of an indecisive chart pattern.

Having decided that we will not take action at the point reached by the share price in Figure 5.1, we can wait for it to unfold a bit further to the position shown in Figure 5.4. Now the share price has turned down again, giving us an important resistance level which the price failed to penetrate on this first attempt. Thus we take no action until the price rises above this level in the future. Naturally, as soon as the price starts to rise again from this current fall we start to take notice, because the price may now be setting out on the upward leg which will penetrate this resistance level. As

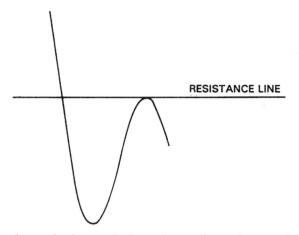
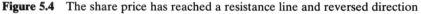

RESISTANCE LINE

Figure 5.4   The share price has reached a resistance line and reversed direction

well as the resistance level noted for the intermediate rise, another important feature will be the position of the second trough which will have been formed once the price starts to rise back towards the resistance level. For the formation to be considered to be a double bottom the second trough should be within 3% of the price at the first trough.

There are now two possibilities, firstly that the price will not rise this far before falling again, and secondly that the price will pass through the resistance level. These two possibilities are shown in Figure 5.5. If the first possibility occurs, then what we have happening is that the share price is still in a downtrend. This can be visualised by drawing a trendline through the two successive peaks. Quite obviously, since the second peak is lower than the first peak, then the trend is still downwards. If the price moves above the first peak, then the trend is upwards, since any subsequent peak that will be formed must be at a higher level than this first peak.

This move of the price above the resistance level, being a sign that an uptrend is now in being, is a signal to buy the share.

Another possibility which will preclude a buy even if the price rises through the resistance level is that the second trough which is formed is not within 3% of the price of the first trough, i.e. the formation does not pass the first test for a double bottom. This leads to two further possibilities: either the second trough is much higher than the first trough, or it is much lower. If the trough is higher, then it is permissible to draw a trendline through these two troughs, and this trendline will slope upwards. We are therefore in an uptrend, and so the investor can consider buying that share. If, on the other hand, the second trough is lower, then there are two further possibilities: either we are still in a downtrend or we are entering an inverted head and shoulders reversal pattern. The first two of these possibilities are shown in Figure 5.6.

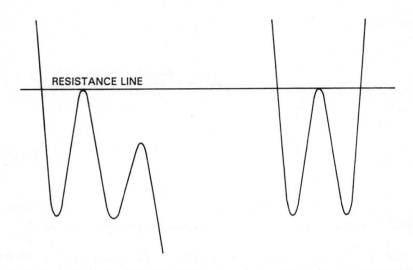

Figure 5.5 On rebounding from the second trough, the price may fail to rise to the previous resistance line, i.e. may now be entering a downtrend. Alternatively, it may rise through the resistance line to form a double bottom

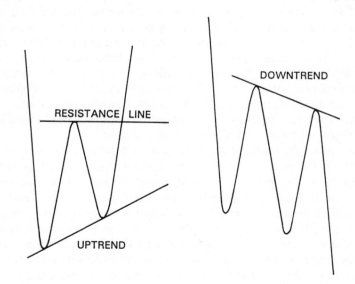

Figure 5.6 The second trough may be higher than the first, in which case the share may be entering an uptrend (left). Alternatively, if the second trough is lower than the first, the price may be entering a downtrend (right)

Now supposing that the share has passed the first test for a double bottom, i.e. the second trough is within 3% of the price of the first trough, then all depends upon whether or not the price continues to rise above the resistance level created by the first peak. If it does, all well and good, because we now have a complete double bottom formation and the share price has now reversed direction to enter a new uptrend. This is now a signal to buy the share.

If, on the other hand, the price retreats again, then the possibility arises that we are seeing a triple bottom formation. The crucial determining factor for this is the position of the third trough. If it is within 3% of either of the two previous troughs, then we are on course for a triple bottom, and all that remains is for the share price to rise above the resistance level formed by the previous two peaks. This will be the signal to buy since the trend reversal pattern is now complete. If the share price does not rise through the resistance level then the direction of the trend is not resolved and the share should be left alone. These possibilities are shown in Figure 5.7.

If the third trough is not within 3% of the level of the previous two troughs, then the pattern is not a triple bottom. If this third trough is higher than the previous two, then it is possible that the trend direction has already been reversed, and we have what can be viewed as a distorted inverted head and shoulders with an upward sloping neckline. This will be confirmed by a rise in price through the previous resistance level. If the third trough is lower than the level of the two previous ones, then the share price is still in a downtrend, and it should be left alone.

Notice the importance of decision making at each stage of the pattern as it unfolds, the failure or success of the share price in reaching support or

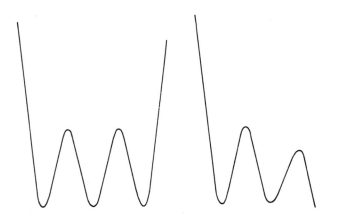

Figure 5.7 If the second trough is at a similar level to the first, then a triple bottom formation is a strong possibility (left). If this is not the case, the pattern is unresolved (right)

Table 5.1 Possible outcomes from a falling share price

Position	Action	Possible formation
After first trough	Price continues to rise	Single bottom
	Price forms a peak and then falls	Double bottom Triple bottom Inverted head and shoulders Downtrend Uptrend
After first peak	Price falls below first trough before rising	Inverted head and shoulders Downtrend
	Price rises from level of first trough	Double bottom Triple bottom
	Price fails to reach level of first trough	Uptrend
After second trough	Price rises past level of first peak	Double bottom
	Price falls after reaching level of first peak	Triple bottom Inverted head and shoulders
	Price fails to reach level of first peak	Downtrend
After second peak	Price falls to level of first trough and then rises	Triple bottom
	Price falls below level of second trough and then rises	Downtrend
	Price fails to reach level of second trough before rising	Uptrend (distorted inverted head and shoulders)

resistance levels leading to several possibilities for the eventual pattern which is formed. These various possibilities are summed up in Table 5.1.

The topping patterns such as single top, double top, triple top, and head and shoulders can be treated in just the same way as the bottoming patterns. Once the price has fallen back from the first peak, the point at which it starts to rise again will now be a support level. It will be the fall of the price down through this support level which will indicate that the future trend is firmly downwards. If the next peak is within 3% of the position of the first peak, then the pattern could turn out to be either a double top or a triple top. If the price falls from this second peak down through the resistance level then a double top has been formed, while if the price bounces back from the support level a triple top will be formed if the price reaches a peak similar to the previous two peaks before falling back down through the support level. Where the second peak is at a higher level than the outer two peaks then of course we have a head and shoulders formation. Any other possibilities will mean that the future direction of the trend is not

Table 5.2 Possible outcomes from a rising share price

Position	Action	Possible formation
After first peak	Price continues to fall	Single top
	Price forms a trough and then rises	Double top Triple top Head and shoulders Downtrend Uptrend

After first trough	Price rises above first peak before
	    falling
		Head and
		    shoulders
		Uptrend

	Price falls from level of first peak	Double top Triple top
	Price fails to reach level of first peak	Downtrend
After second peak	Price falls past level of first trough	Double top

	Price rises after reaching level of first
	    trough
		Triple top
		Head and
		    shoulders

	Price fails to reach level of first trough	Uptrend
After second trough	Price rises to level of first peak and then falls	Triple top
	Price rises above level of second peak and then falls	Uptrend
	Price fails to reach level of second peak before falling	Downtrend (distorted head and shoulders)

resolved. In such cases to assume that the future direction of the share price is down may be incorrect.

The various possibilities for topping formations as the share price unfolds are shown in Table 5.2.

At this point it is necessary to draw attention once again to the distinction between bottoming patterns as a basis for buying shares and topping patterns as a basis for selling shares. Once a reversal pattern has been completed, the balance of probabilities is such that the new trend in the share price should be moving in the opposite direction. What leads to the difficulty is that the pattern is not completed until the price has pulled away from the previous resistance level in the case of bottoming patterns, and fallen below the support level in the case of topping patterns. The resistance level can be some way, perhaps 10 or 20%, above the bottom price, while the support level can be a similar way below the top price. Now to give up the first 10 or 20% of a price rise is perfectly permissible when we look at the broader picture in which the rise may well take the share price to double its low value. It is not permissible to stay on board a share price which falls back by this amount from the top price. After all, there is no guarantee that the price will not suddenly plummet at any point between its top value and the support level, giving a huge, unacceptable loss.

It must be emphasised, therefore, that topping patterns must not be used as criteria for selling a share. Shares should be sold because they have fallen below a stop loss level, or because one of the indicators discussed later in this book is signalling that the trend has turned downwards.

6

Bottoming Patterns

Psychologically, investors are much more interested in the buying of shares than the selling of shares, even though the buying and selling decisions are equally important, since many good buying decisions have been ruined by a failure to sell at the right time. For the investor focused on buying, a recognition of the various types of bottoming patterns which can get him into a share early in its new upward trend is of prime interest.

Because of the sustained bull market over the last decade, there is a shortage of examples of the major bottoming formations, but plenty of the major topping formations. Even so, there are enough examples of bottoming formations to illustrate how they can be used in a practical sense.

SINGLE BOTTOM FORMATIONS

As we pointed out in the last chapter, the simplest bottoming formation is the single bottom. This can occur as either a sharp bottom or a rounded bottom. In the case of a sharp bottom, the rapid reaction of the share price is such that an investor is rarely in a position to take advantage of it. A large proportion of the upward movement takes place over such a short time that the potential for further gain becomes limited. This is not a problem with a rounded bottom formation, which can take many months for its completion. The different problem with the rounded bottom formation, as was discussed in the last chapter, is at what level it is appropriate to make an investment. The author's view, expressed earlier, is that the rounded bottom formation is best left alone as an investment opportunity unless one or other of the indicators discussed later in this book is signalling that a rise is in the offing.

A good example of a rounded bottom formation is shown in Figure 6.1 for GEC. The formation took about a year to complete, the lowest point of 144p being reached in April 1988. One way in which the rounded bottom can be highlighted as it develops is by drawing a succession of trendlines between successive important troughs. These should become less steep as

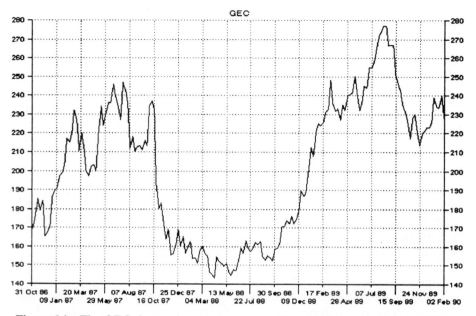

Figure 6.1 The GEC share price shows a rounded bottom formation during 1988

the bottom of the pattern is approached, and then begin to increase in slope again.

It is extremely difficult to find a perfect example of a rounded bottom, and the one in Figure 6.1 is no exception. Thus the pattern is slightly spoiled by the fact that the price in September 1988 dipped below the trough reached at the end of July. This small fall was only temporary, and the price soon re-established its curved upward trend.

It is not necessary to use trendlines to highlight the rounded bottom formation. The outline of the rounded bottom can easily be obtained by drawing as smooth a curve as possible through the number of troughs which were formed from the beginning of 1988, as has been done in Figure 6.2. The solid line shows how this would have been done at the time that the trough in early June was formed, while the dotted line shows how the future course of the rounded bottom was estimated. The fact that the price violated this projected curve in August/September forms a useful basis for deciding on how the pattern would be treated as a buying opportunity for those investors who ignore the advice above about using indicators to generate a buying signal. An idea of what constitutes a viable buying level can be obtained by drawing a number of levels on the chart at increasing percentage movement from the bottom level. Since this level was 144p, lines are drawn at 10% higher (158.5p), 15% higher (165.5p) and 20% higher (173p). These values are rounded to the nearest 0.5p.

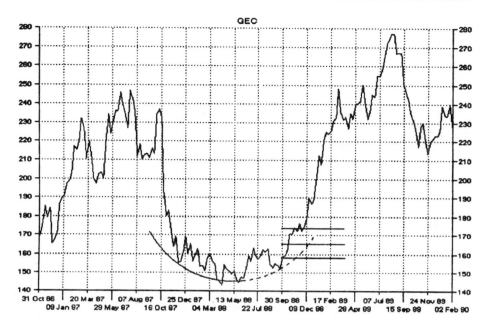

Figure 6.2 The rounded bottom is now projected into the future. The horizontal lines show levels of 10%, 15% and 20% up from the trough price

As it was being formed, the trough at 155p at the end of August could have been the start of a decline, and there was no evidence either way to support the fact that the rounded bottom would continue or fail. An investor using a 10% level up from the bottom price would therefore have been at risk, since this buying level would have been triggered at the end of June, leaving him feeling quite nervous for the next three months. Another way of looking at things is that capital would have been tied up unnecessarily in a non-performing situation. Thus we can come to the conclusion, from this example, that the 10% level is not sufficiently above the base price for the curved uptrend to have become definitely established.

We now have to find another level such that there is still sufficient potential for gain, but with decreased risk. The 20% level does not satisfy this requirement, since the price level would then be 173p, which would look quite high from the historical perspective. On the other hand, the 15% level would have prevented us investing too soon, while leaving the possibility of a decent rise to come. For those investors who wish to take advantage of a rounded bottom formation, a buying level of 15% up from the lowest price reached is usually safe.

Sometimes a rounded bottoming formation can take many years to complete. An example is the Dixons share price following the crash of

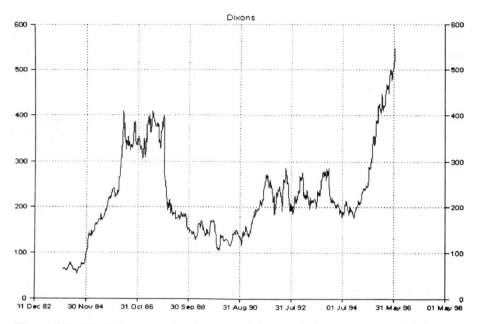

Figure 6.3 The Dixons share price passed through a long term rounded bottom formation during 1989 and 1990

1987. The chart in Figure 6.3 shows that the bottom began immediately after the crash in October 1987, and continued to June 1991 before entering a period of see-saw movement within a trading range of 200p to 280p. This latter type of movement in what is called a rectangle is discussed later in the chapter on hesitation patterns. These usually result in an extensive breakout as can be seen in the meteoric rise to about 550p.

An enlarged view of the rounded bottom part of the Dixons price movement is shown in more detail in Figure 6.4. A central curved trendline drawn through this formation illustrates quite clearly the saucer-like trend, with the short term movements making excursions only about 20p above or below this central trend. The trend can be said to have ended when a price excursion from the projected trend exceeds this 20p threshold by, say, a further 10p. A better way of looking at these saucer bottoming patterns is to imagine them as an arc of a circle. If the centre point of the circle is established, then the curved trend can be readily drawn with the aid of a pair of compasses or by computer. The trend will run out of steam normally when the arc has reached a quarter of the circle.

The practical aspect of such long drawn out patterns is that the rate of increase is normally too slow for them to be a good investment. The use of the arc of a circle method does allow an investor who is already invested in that share to take a view on when to get out.

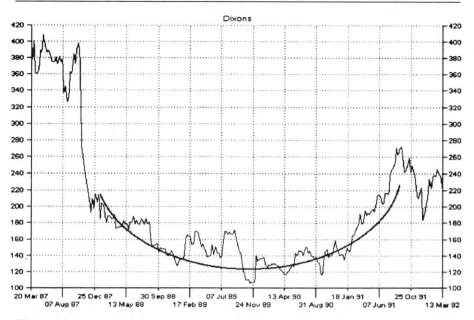

Figure 6.4 An enlarged view of the rounded bottom in the Dixons share price. If the central trend is taken to be the arc of a circle, then this rarely extends to more than a quadrant

Usually, much better investment opportunities than those provided by rounded bottom formations can be found by the alert chartist.

DOUBLE BOTTOM FORMATIONS

These formations are rarely symmetrical, and the time gap between the two bottoms can also vary considerably. As a general rule, the levels reached by the two legs of the double bottom should be within 3% of each other. In many cases, the two legs are within a penny or so of each other. The chart of Lloyds the Chemists in Figure 6.5 shows a double bottom pattern in which the two bottoms are over two and a half years apart. The first, on 25th September 1992, was at a level of 185p, while the second, on 31st March 1995, reached a floor of 188p. Thus the levels reached by the two legs differed by only about 1.6%. Both bottoms are fairly sharp, i.e. the price did not spend more than a few weeks below the 200p level.

In Figure 6.6 we can see the chart of Siebe in which the two bottoms are just under four months apart. The first leg reached a level of 504p on 5th October 1994, while the second one, on 31st January 1995, was at a level of 499p, i.e. a difference of only 1%. As with Lloyds the Chemists, the share price rose strongly from the second low point, posting a gain of about 60% during the following year.

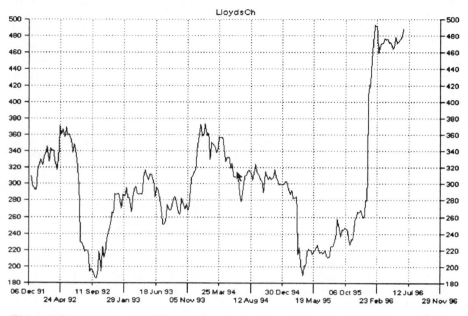

Figure 6.5 A long term double bottom in the Lloyds the Chemists share price. The two legs are over two years apart

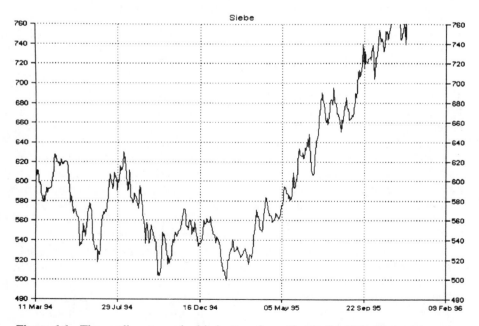

Figure 6.6 The medium term double bottom formation in the Siebe share price

Guardian Royal Exchange also showed a medium term double bottom (Figure 6.7). A closer inspection shows that the first leg of the double bottom was itself a very short term double bottom. The price fell to 164p on 30th May 1994, rose to 182p over the next three weeks and then fell sharply back to 162p on 24th June. It took another six months before the price came back to these levels, reaching a low of 161p on 23rd January 1995. Such cases, where the two legs of the bottom are very close together, as was the case in May/June 1994, have to be watched very carefully. In general, the closer together the two legs, the less is the subsequent rise from this position. Thus investors may make little or no profit from such formations. In the present case the rise took the price to around the 190p mark, generating a small profit. On the other hand, the leg in January 1995 was the one that saw a large subsequent rise of more than 100p.

The criterion to use in those cases where the two legs of a double bottom are very close together is to view it as a single bottom formation. As discussed in the previous section, the critical level for buying after a single bottom is when the price has moved up by more than 15% from the bottom. Thus in the GRE case, the buying level following the first bottom of 164p in May 1994 would be 188.5p. The price reached this level in the middle of July, but made very little progress after that, reaching only 201p before falling back.

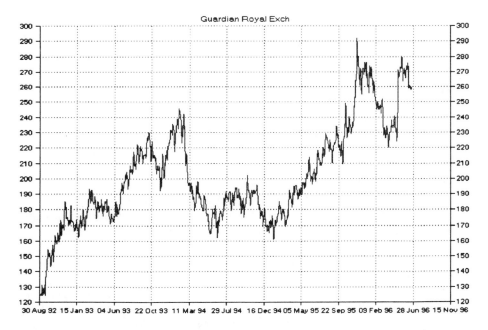

Figure 6.7   The medium term double bottom formation in the GRE share price

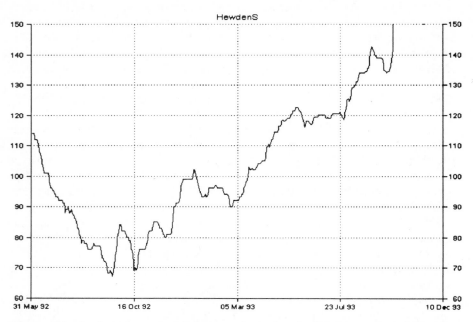

Figure 6.8 A short term double bottom formation in the share price of Hewden Stuart

A final example of a double bottom with two legs very close together is that of Hewden Stuart, shown in Figure 6.8. Here the first leg reached a minimum on 16th September 1992, rose to 84p by 25th September, and then fell back to 69p on 15th October before rising from that level to make a very useful gain.

TRIPLE BOTTOM FORMATIONS

These are somewhat rarer than double bottom formations, probably because many triple bottoms become distorted into inverse head and shoulders patterns by the centre bottom being considerably lower than the outer two. Even when this is not the case, a perfectly symmetrical triple bottom is very rare. As discussed in the theoretical section, the asymmetry can be either in the distance apart of the three troughs, or in the fact that the two intermediate peaks do not rise to the same level.

The chart of Barclays Banks in Figure 6.9 shows an asymmetry in the distance apart of the three legs of the formation. The bottoms are very sharp troughs: 502p on 9th March 1994, 499p on 4th May 1994, and 500p on 1st June 1994. Thus the gap between the first two legs is about eight weeks, and that between the second and third legs is just under four weeks.

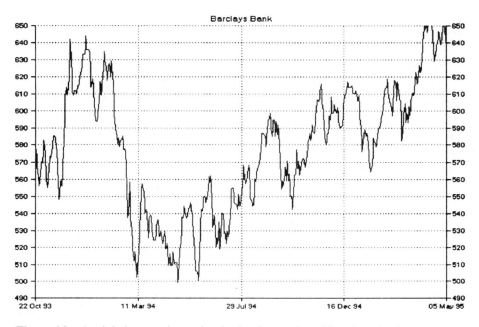

Figure 6.9 A triple bottom formation in the share price of Barclays Bank

The troughs all occur within 3p of each other, i.e. within less than 1%. Although at first sight the intermediate peaks would appear to be at markedly different levels, this is a perception caused by the scaling being used. The first peak, on 16th March, reached 557p, while the peak between the second and third legs reached 546p. Thus these two peaks are still within about 2% of each other, close enough to avoid being labelled as asymmetric.

Asymmetry in the height of the intermediate peaks can cause a problem if the second intermediate peak is higher than the first. The problem lies in the fact that once the second peak has passed the level of the first peak, the formation takes on the appearance of a double bottom, encouraging the investor to buy once the price has risen above this first level. Thus there needs to be a small tolerance built in. A good policy here is to wait for the price to rise by some 3% above the previous peak level before buying. While not eliminating all occasions where what appears to be a double bottom is actually a triple bottom, it will reduce these considerably.

An example where the investor would still have been in the wrong even when applying this 3% rule can be seen in the case of Great Portland, in Figure 6.10. The first trough in mid-August 1992 fell to 96p, and the price then rose to a temporary peak of 110p in mid-September. This is marginally below our buying level of 15% up from the trough, i.e. a level of 110.4p, so that an investor thinking that the previous trough was a single

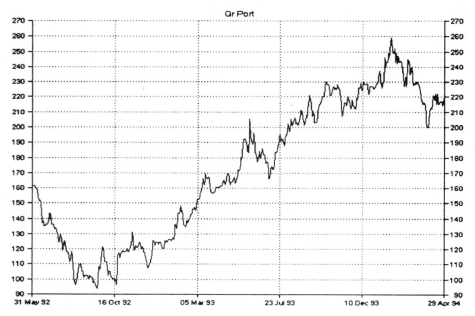

Figure 6.10   A triple bottom formation in the share price of Great Portland

bottom formation would not be buying the share. The price then fell back again to 93p before rising again.

Now we see the danger of an asymmetry, since the price rose to 121p. An investor could have got in at 114p on the way to this peak, i.e. once the 3% level above the previous peak of 110p had been passed, but the price of 121p represented the best achieved for a few weeks. A stop loss would have got the investor out of the false double bottom with just a small loss.

Since quadruple bottoms are quite rare, i.e. false triple bottoms are rare, then a rise out of the third bottom would be seen to be very positive, since the investor would be unlikely to be caught in the same trap as occurred with the false double bottom.

Asymmetry in which the second intermediate peak is not as high as the first one does not cause a problem, since the investor would not buy after the second trough due to the failure of the price to pass the level of the first intermediate peak, i.e. the position following the second trough does not meet the buying criteria by surpassing the first peak by at least 3%. An example of this is to be found in Guardian Royal Exchange in 1986, as shown in Figure 6.11.

The first bottom occurred on 26th September 1986 at a price of 153p. The price rose to an intermediate peak of 165.5p by the end of October before falling back again to a level of 151.5p. Although the rise to 153.5p over the next week would have suggested that the price was now rising

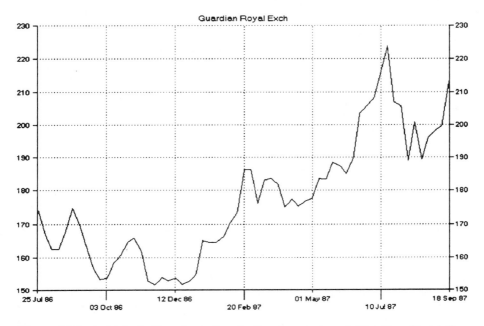

Figure 6.11 A triple bottom formation in the share price of Guardian Royal Exchange (weekly data)

from the second trough of a double bottom formation, the investor would have been waiting for a rise at least 3% above the previous peak of 165.5p. Instead, the price fell back again to the previous trough of 151.5p before rising again. Once more, the investor would be waiting to clear the 165.5p level by a good 3%, i.e. to pass a level of 170p. This happened on 6th February 1987, at which point the investor could have bought with the probability of a useful rise. As can be seen from the chart, the price made a significant improvement to over 220p by July that year.

THE INVERTED HEAD AND SHOULDERS FORMATION

Inverted head and shoulders formations are fairly common during bear markets, but there are not so many examples over the last five years or so because of the underlying bull market for shares in general. The formation can take many weeks or even many years to complete. A typical example is shown in Figure 6.12 for Courtaulds, which lasted just over six months.

At the beginning of the pattern, the price fell to a low point of 224p in September 1988, and bounced back from this level. The crucial level of 15% up from this at 258p was not reached, and so the investor would do

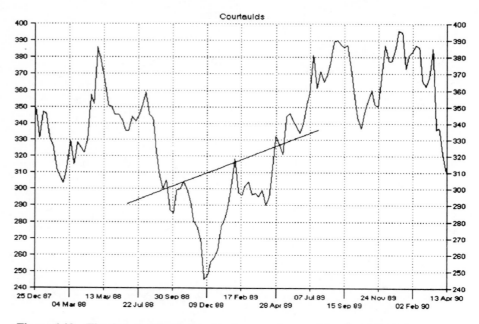

Figure 6.12 The Courtaulds share price shows an inverted head and shoulders around the low point in December 1988

nothing but continue to keep an eye on the developing pattern. The fall from this point took the price well below its previous trough of 224p to the 200p level. Not unexpectedly, since this is a 'round number' level, the price bounced back again. The investor would now begin to think in terms of a possible head and shoulders, since this second peak is well below the tolerance of within 3% of the level of the previous peak necessary for a double bottom formation. The price then rose steadily, passing the 245p level of the previous peak, reaching 255p before retracing again. The level reached by the two intermediate peaks is of course the neckline of the inverted head and shoulders, and would be horizontal for a perfectly symmetrical formation. In this present case, the neckline is therefore sloping upwards, but not at such a slope that the formation would cease to be considered an inverted head and shoulders. Note that a line joining the shoulders, i.e. joining the two troughs either side of the main trough, is more or less at the same slope as the neckline. When the slopes of these two lines are markedly dissimilar, the pattern cannot really be described as a meaningful inverted head and shoulders.

The formation is not completed until the rise from the second shoulder, i.e. from a level of 240p in this case, takes the price above the neckline, i.e. above 255p. This happened in May 1989. The normal prediction for the rise in price from this point at which the neckline is broken is for an amount similar to the price difference between the lowest point of the central peak, i.e. 200p, to the right-hand neckline, i.e. 255p. This should therefore take the price to about 310p. This forecast was uncannily correct, since the price reached 312p before falling back again.

The chart of Slough Estates, shown in Figure 6.13, is extremely interesting since it shows two inverted head and shoulders formations nested one inside the other around the low point in early August 1992. The two necklines are shown in the figure. The first is at a level of around 200p, gently sloping upwards from left to right, and the second, sloping similarly, is at a level of about 280p. Note once again that the predicted price rise for the inner inverted head and shoulders is correct within a few percent. The rise from the low point of 100p to the neckline of approximately 200p is about 100p. We would therefore expect a rise of a further 100p to about 300p. As can be seen from the chart, the price reached 288p before retracing.

The completion of the outer of the two patterns still has some way to go, since the latest price in the chart, in the middle of the developing shoulder, at about 236p, still has some way to go to reach the level of the neckline at 280p. It is from this point that a rise would be expected, and using the same criteria as before, we would expect this rise to take the price the same distance above the neckline that the neckline is above the central trough,

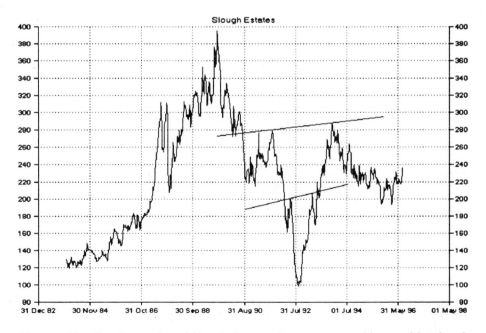

Figure 6.13 The share price of Slough Estates shows two nested inverted head and shoulders around the low point in August 1992. The inner has a neckline at 200p, while the outer has a neckline at about 280p

i.e. a rise of about 180p. This would take the price to around 460p, comfortably passing the previous high of 398p.

The chart of Ward Holdings in Figure 6.14 is a perfect example of a horizontal neckline, which in this case is at 55p. The pattern is marred somewhat by the distorted nature of the shoulders. The left-hand one descends to 40p, with a large short term rise to 54p in the middle of it, while the right-hand shoulder descends to 34p. On the basis of the rules for a subsequent price rise, the rise from the trough to the neckline is about 40p, and therefore the anticipated level to which the price should rise from the neckline is about 95p. The actual price rise was to a level of 72p, which although less than anticipated, still represents a useful profit of 30% for the investor who got in as the price passed the previous neckline.

BUYING RULES

1. First trough   If the price rises by 15% from the lowest point, then the formation is probably a rounded bottom and the investor can buy.

2. Second trough   If the price at the second trough is within 3% of that of the first trough then the formation is either a double bottom or a triple

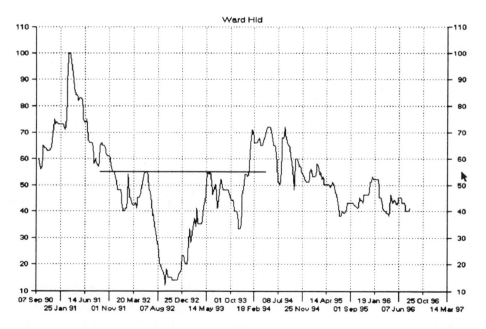

Figure 6.14   The share price of Ward Holdings shows an inverted head and shoulders pattern in which each shoulder is somewhat distorted

bottom. If the price then rises above the level of the peak price between the first and second troughs, the formation is a double bottom and the investor can buy, otherwise wait for triple bottom pattern development.

3. Second trough   If the price at the second trough is lower than that of the first trough, then the formation is probably an inverted head and shoulders. Wait for pattern development.

4. Third trough   If the price level at the third trough is within 3% of that of the first trough, then a triple bottom or head and shoulders is probable. If a triple bottom, wait for the price to rise above the level of the higher of the two intermediate peaks before buying. If an inverted head and shoulders, wait for the price to rise above the neckline (the line joining the tops of the two intermediate peaks) before buying.

5. Third trough   If the price level at the third trough is not within 3% of that of the first trough, move to another share.

7

Topping Patterns

Unlike the situation with bottoming patterns, charts of the last 10 years of share price histories are rich with examples of topping patterns. There are many instances of single tops, rounded tops, double tops, triple tops and head and shoulders. Even so, a perfect symmetrical example of any of these patterns is still rare, and there are usually slight differences from perfection. The approach to these topping patterns is virtually a mirror image of that employed for the bottoming formations, with similar rules being employed about the extent to which a price should fall back from the top, how close together multiple tops have to be, etc.

SINGLE TOP FORMATIONS

All rounded top formations, and indeed all rounded bottom formations, will be slightly distorted by the presence of fluctuations of much shorter duration than the formation itself. A good example is that of Allied Domecq, shown in Figure 7.1. Here we have a rounded top that took six years for its completion. A line drawn so as to touch the minor peaks that occur between the end of April 1990 and July 1996 is obviously a rounded curve. Instead of such a curve, it is also possible to draw fan lines, which exhibit a gradual reduction in their slopes until the slopes change direction as the top of the formation is passed. The lines then get increasingly steep again. The clean pattern is rather spoilt by the large fall that occurred some weeks before the steep rise to the peak of 669p on 7th January 1994, but even so, this extreme peak is only slightly above the smooth line that can be drawn.

As far as the extent of a fall from a rounded top formation is concerned, for a symmetrical top the expectation has to be for a fall to the general level of the share price before the rise to the top occurred. In this case, therefore, the level of 423p reached in July 1996 is close enough to the starting level of 412p in April 1990 that the formation can be assumed to be at an end, and that a rise from the current level should occur.

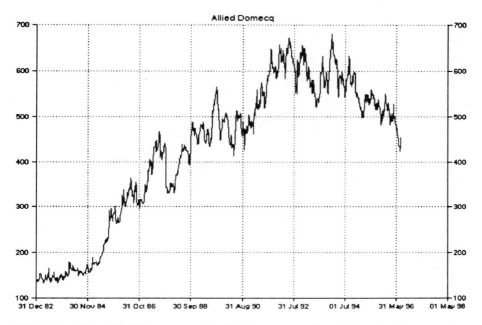

Figure 7.1 The Allied Domecq share price shows a number of very short term cycles superimposed on a rounded top formation

A rounded top taking much less time for its completion than the six years in the previous example is that of Severn Trent Water, as shown in Figure 7.2. This formation started in mid-1995 and appeared to be completed by mid-1996, i.e. it took about a year for completion. The smooth top was interrupted slightly by a reverse earthquake formation, i.e. a near-vertical rise (September 1995) followed some time later by a near-vertical fall (from the peak of 688p in January 1996). This feature of the short term rises and falls becoming more extreme as the top is approached seems to be characteristic of most rounded tops, as we also saw in the previous example.

These two examples show the difficulty with rounded top formations—perfectly symmetrical ones are quite rare, and ones which look good bets for behaving perfectly usually show an erratic behaviour just after the top has passed, and usually before the fall of 15% is reached. For this reason, and this has been stated many times, investors are not encouraged to take major investment decisions based simply on a developing rounded top pattern. This comment is really aimed at traded options investors, since an investor in shares must use a stop loss method to generate a selling signal, and not wait for any of the topping formations to be completed.

Rolls-Royce, shown in Figure 7.3, is another case in point of a rounded top suffering increasing short term movements as the top is approached.

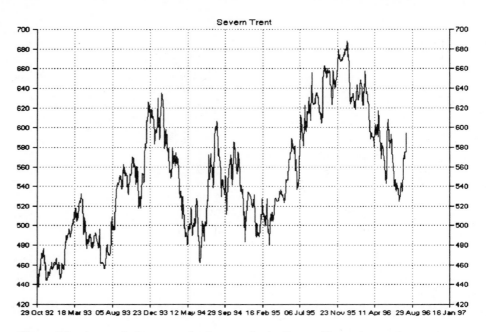

Figure 7.2   A rounded top can also be seen in the Severn Trent share price

From the symmetry point of view, we have to consider that the top began somewhere around November 1993 and finished at the low point of 152p in March 1995. The extreme movement at the top was interesting because it generated a double top formation, i.e. we have a rounded top with a double top superimposed on it. The first leg of the double top occurred on 29th April 1994 at a level of 203.5p. The price then fell to an intermediate low of 174p on 24th June 1994 before rising to the second leg of the top on 26th August 1994 at 202.5p, just a penny shy of the previous leg. Thus the short term movements at the top result in a swing of nearly 30p, whereas earlier and later in the rounded top formation the swings are more of the order of 15p or so.

DOUBLE TOP FORMATIONS

There are many examples of double tops to be found over the last few years. The patterns can be long term, in the sense that the tops are more than a year apart, or they can be relatively short term, the tops being but a few weeks apart. The main criterion is that the price levels of the two tops should be within 3% of each other.

The Cable & Wireless share price as shown in Figure 7.4 is an excellent example of a long term double top, the two tops being about three years

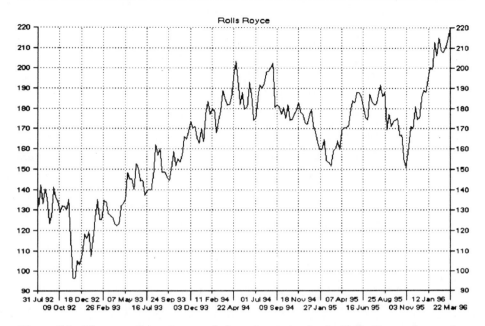

Figure 7.3 The symmetry of a rounded top formation in the Rolls-Royce share price is disturbed by the superimposed double top in mid-1994

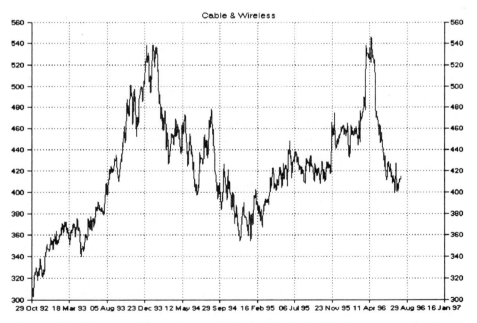

Figure 7.4 The rounded top formation in the Cable & Wireless share price has a sharp top formation superimposed on it

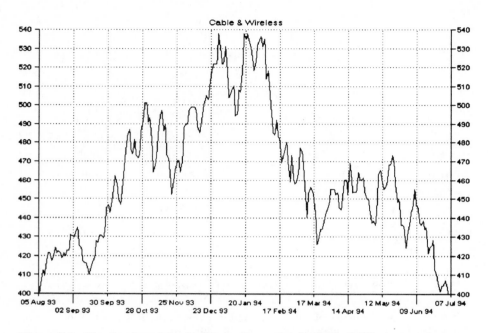

Figure 7.5 The first leg of the double top formation in Cable & Wireless can be seen to be a multiple top when the chart is expanded

apart in time. It also has the intriguing aspect that the first leg on the double top can be seen to be a short term multiple top, as shown in the expanded chart in Figure 7.5.

The classic condition of a good run up in the share price is present, since the price moved from around 340p in March 1993 to a peak level of 538p on 29th December 1993. The price fell back to 494p in mid-January 1994 before making another attempt at the peak. This reached 538p once again, on 19th January, before falling once more. The final attempt took the price to 536.5p on 4th February 1994 before falling rapidly to the 430p level. Note again the classic situation as regards the fall back from the final peak. The normal expectation is for a fall at least as far below the level of the intermediate trough as the trough is below the peak. Since the trough is at 494p, and therefore 44p down from the peak, we would expect the fall to be at least 44p down from the trough, i.e. at 494p – 44p = 450p. The fall to 430p is even greater than the expectation.

Coming back to the long term double top as shown in Figure 7.4, it took another two years before the next attempt on the previous peak of 538p occurred. The 538p level was reached on 1st April 1996, with a rapid rise from 477.5p on 27th March, and a further attempt enabled the share to pass this point to reach 546p a few weeks later.

The price fell quite rapidly back to 479p by May. This second leg of the long term double bottom can be seen to be a reverse earthquake, in which the initial rapid rise of 68.5p in just a few days is matched by a fall of a similar amount, again in the space of a few days.

An example of a short term double top is shown by the Sears share price in Figure 7.6. The rise to the top of the first leg was very rapid, the price rising from 130p to 175p in just a few weeks in July 1987. The price then fell back to an intermediate trough of 159p before rising once again to 175.5p on 2nd October. This was just two weeks before the October 1987 crash, but note that there were warning signs, since the price fell back from this peak over the two weeks before the crash. Thus an astute investor would have taken the failure to pass the previous peak decisively as a negative sign, and would have come out of the share.

General Accident is another example of a short term double top (Figure 7.7), although the levels the individual legs reached are rather further apart than in the previous examples. The price reached 731p on 15th October 1993 before falling back to an intermediate trough of 633p. On the next attempt the price passed the previous high, climbing to 752p on 7th January 1994. The peaks are still within 3% of each other, thus qualifying as a double top. Since the trough was approximately 119p below the later of the two peaks, the target area into which the price should fall is 633p − 119p = 514p. The price fell initially to a level of 541p on 1st July

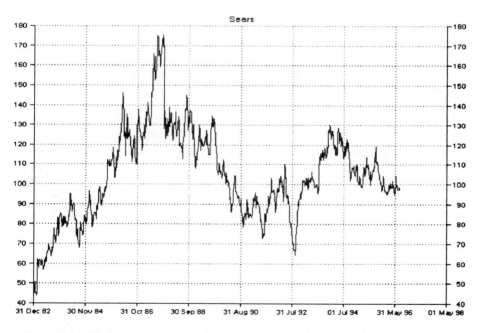

Figure 7.6 The Sears share price shows a short term double top in 1986

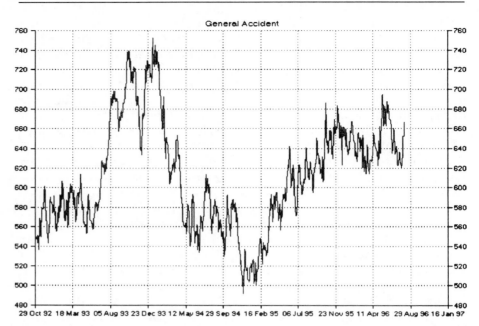

• **Figure 7.7** The share price of General Accident shows a short term double top formation in late 1993

1994, rather less than anticipated, but this was only a temporary halt to the decline, since by the end of the year the price had bottomed out at 505p.

Finally, another example of a short term double top can be seen in the Lonrho share price as shown in Figure 7.8. The first leg reached 217p before falling back to an intermediate trough of 189p. The price then rose to 216p before starting a decline which took the price down to 165p, lower than the anticipated level of 172p.

Naturally, there are many occasions where the price does not fall to the anticipated distance below the intermediate peak, even when everything seems to be correct for a normal double top pattern—there is a good rise to the first peak, the intermediate trough is still some way above the original starting level, and the second peak is within 3% of the level of the first peak. It can still happen that the fall from the second peak takes the price only marginally below the level of the intermediate trough before rising again. Even so, on the balance of probabilities, a well-defined double top formation should lead to a significant fall in the share price.

TRIPLE TOP FORMATIONS

A perfectly symmetrical triple top formation is extremely rare. Most triple tops become distorted into a head and shoulders pattern, but examples of triple tops with lesser distortion do exist.

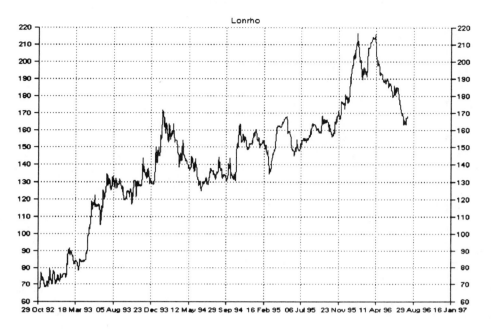

Figure 7.8 A good example of a short term double top in Lonrho

The four requirements for a perfect triple top are:

- The price should have risen substantially
- The levels of the tops should be within 3% of each other
- The intermediate troughs should be at similar levels
- The three peaks should be equally spaced in time

The first two of these are essential if the pattern is to be considered a triple top. Most triple top formations will fail to satisfy either the third or fourth requirement, and some will fail on both of these.

A good example of a triple top that satisfies the first two requirements is to be found with Reckitt & Coleman, as shown in Figure 7.9. The pattern is a medium term one, the three peaks occurring over the course of one year, between July 1995 and June 1996. From some points of view the share could be said to exhibit a multiple top, since there is a previous peak in December 1993 that reached a similar level.

As far as the actual triple top is concerned, the price had risen substantially from just above 620p to 711p by late July 1995. The intermediate trough between the first two peaks was at 635p. On the middle leg, the price reached 722p before falling back to the second trough at 621p. The final leg took the price up to 728p in June 1996.

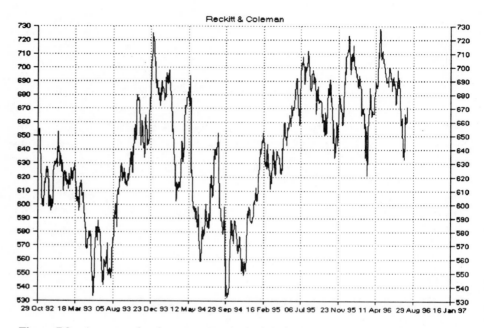

Figure 7.9   An example of an asymmetrical triple top in Reckitt and Coleman

Although the levels reached by the three peaks are increasing from left to right, they cover a range of 711p to 728p. The difference is still within 2.4%, less than the 3% maximum spread.

At the time of writing the pattern is still not complete. The expected level to which the price should fall from the third peak is about 540p, using the criterion of a fall to a similar distance below the second intermediate trough that the third peak is above it. This would bring the price down to the resistance levels seen in June 1993 and September 1994, giving added weight to the prediction.

Another example of a triple top is to be found in PowerGen, as shown in Figure 7.10. Although this is a long term topping pattern, since the formation lasted from July 1994 to April 1996, the levels reached by the three peaks are remarkably close. These were 600p for the first leg, 604p for the second leg and 605p for the third leg, i.e. within less than 1%, far less than the 3% criterion for a triple top. The formation is, however, asymmetric, since the first trough between peaks one and two descends to 465p, while the second is at the higher level of 508p, a considerable difference.

The fall subsequent to the third peak was less than anticipated, coming down to 465p rather than around 410p, but at the time of writing the pattern is not yet quite resolved.

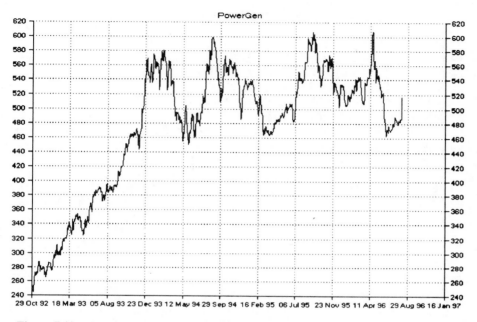

Figure 7.10   Another example of a triple top, in PowerGen

MULTIPLE TOPS

Occasionally patterns can be seen which have more than three peaks at about the same price level. These are best referred to as multiple tops. Symmetrical examples where all troughs are at the same general level and the peaks are equally spaced in time are virtually never seen. Interestingly, the previous example of PowerGen contained a multiple top as well as the triple top just discussed. This is the formation seen in early 1994. Five peaks can be seen that fall between 563p and 579p, i.e. covering a range of 2.8%, just within the 3% criterion. As with the triple top, the fall from the final peak is within expectation.

A more obvious example is to be found in the chart of Grand Metropolitan, shown in Figure 7.11. At least eight peaks can be seen in the first half of 1994 which fall between the limits of 480p and 493p, covering a range of 2.7%. There are also four substantial valleys within the group of peaks as well as minor ones. The penultimate peak at 476p can be disregarded since it falls outside this range, and the valley between it and the last peak is shallow. It does fulfil one other criterion, that the price rise entering the formation should be substantial. In this case the price climbed from 379p to 493p (i.e. by 30%) in a matter of weeks. The corresponding fall at the end of the multiple peak sequence took the price all the way back down again.

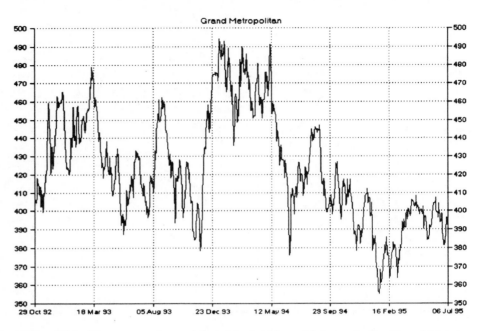

Figure 7.11 There are at least eight peaks in this multiple top in the Grand Metropolitan share price

   The chart of Wolseley in Figure 7.12 poses a dilemma, since it can be viewed as a type of rounded top (the group of peaks in early 1996), or a double top, with the first top in March 1994 being a sharp one and the rounded top being the second one of the pair, or even as an example of a multiple top if the rounded top is looked at more closely. In this rounded top, there are five peaks clustered between 478p and 485p (a range of 1.5%) with reasonable valleys between them. While the pattern is not yet completed at the time of writing, there has been a fall back from the top of more than twice the depth of the last valley.

HEAD AND SHOULDERS

Head and shoulders formations are fairly rare compared with the other types of topping formations. They are formed of three tops, the central one being higher than the outside two. The outside peaks are the shoulders, while the neckline is the line joining the two intermediate troughs. The neckline is frequently sloping upwards or downwards rather than horizontal. A perfect formation with a horizontal neckline, equal height shoulders and the head centrally placed between the shoulders is extremely rare. More typical are the examples shown in the following

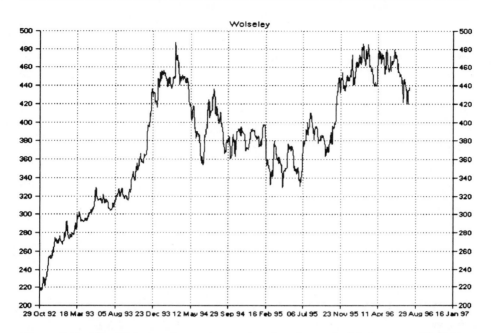

Figure 7.12 The Wolseley share price can be viewed as a double top or multiple top formation

three charts. Figure 7.13 shows such a formation in the chart of Hanson. The neckline is almost perfectly horizontal, but the right-hand shoulder is much lower than the left-hand one. The head is also marred somewhat by the trough on its right-hand side. The usual prediction for the behaviour of the price following the head and shoulders formation is that once it has fallen some 3% below the level of the neckline, then the fall should continue at least as far below the neckline as the top of the head is above it. Since the top of the head is at 292p, and the neckline is at 226p, the target area is therefore about 160p. At the time of writing the price had fallen to this level before making a slight recovery.

In the head and shoulders shown in Figure 7.14 for Slough Estates, we have a neckline that is sloping downwards to the right. Even so, it can be seen that the target area for the price is almost reached. The height of the top of the head above the neckline is about 45p, and with the neckline at 260p, this gives a target of 215p once the price has fallen more than 3% below the neckline. Thus the crucial trigger for a further fall is the fall below 252p.

A sloping neckline going the other way can be seen in the share price of Lloyds the Chemists (Figure 7.15). The unusual feature of this formation is that, taking a longer term view, it took place at levels which turned out to be the lower end of the historic price range rather than at the higher end.

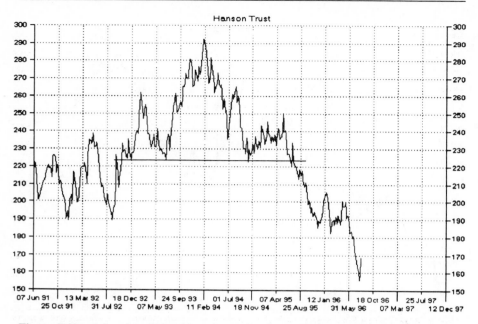

Figure 7.13 A head and shoulders formation in the Hanson share price. While the shoulders are not at equal heights, the neckline shown by the straight line is horizontal

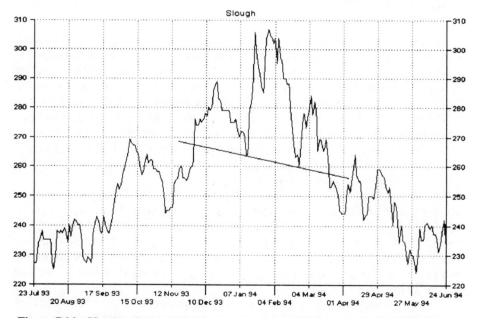

Figure 7.14 Head and shoulders formation in the Slough Estates share price. In this example the neckline is sloping downwards to the right, and the right shoulder is lower than the left one

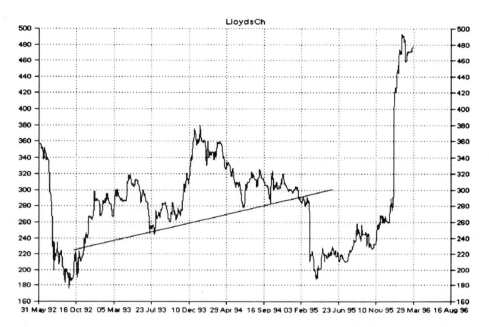

Figure 7.15 A head and shoulders formation in the Lloyds the Chemists share price. In this example the neckline is sloping upwards to the right, but the right shoulder is at a similar level to the left one

It is only in the short term that the formation can be seen to be a topping one, since the price does drop below the neckline and continues down to somewhere around the anticipated levels.

SELLING RULES

In the last chapter a number of buying rules were listed for the various bottoming formations. The logic here was that once the bottoming formation was complete, the investor should be able to look forward to a rise in price, and therefore the situation was one of low risk and high potential for profit. The situation with topping formations is quite different, since by the time they have been completed and the price is in a downtrend the fall from the top is already considerable. A much smaller loss in price from the peak price can be obtained by the use of stop losses. For this reason, no selling rules will be presented here.

8

Trending Patterns

The previous two chapters concerned reversal patterns, where as the pattern unfolds, an upper or lower limit to the price trend becomes obvious. The expectation is then for the price trend to reverse direction. This chapter discusses trending patterns, where as long as the pattern unfolds, the trend is continuing, and the point at which the trend will reverse is unknown. Technical analysis is bedevilled by the misuse of mathematics and indeed the misuse of English. Thus it would be logical to call the trending patterns which will be discussed in this chapter 'continuation patterns', since it is readily established that the trend being examined is continuing. Unfortunately in technical analysis this term has a rather different meaning, and applies to situations where the trend of the price after the pattern is in the same direction as the trend of the price before the pattern rather than applying to the behaviour of the price within the pattern. A much better term for these situations would be 'hesitation patterns', because there is a period of hesitation and uncertainty before the trend is re-established, and the term is self-explanatory.

It seems rather meaningless to state that a trending pattern will continue until it ends, but the point is that we can focus on the pattern in such a way that as soon as it does end, we know that it has ended. We are thus able to take the appropriate investment action at an early stage. The trends discussed in this chapter are of two types: simple trends, both up and down, and trends which are contained within a channel. Either of these types can be straight or curved.

SIMPLE TRENDS

Straight Uptrend

The chart of British American Tobacco in Figure 8.1 is an excellent example of a long term uptrend that has been in being from mid-1985. An uptrend line has to have at least three troughs on or close to it in order to be valid, and this example has some five troughs lying along it.

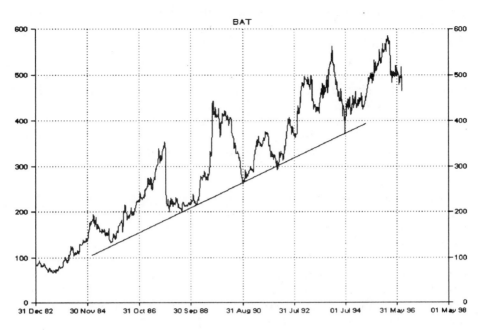

Figure 8.1 BAT provides an excellent example of a long term uptrend. The uptrend is identified by the straight line passing through five troughs in the price

With such a pattern it is obvious that while any new troughs that are formed fall within the allowed tolerance either side of the trendline, the uptrend is still in being, and the investor can ride with it. The key to good profits is of course the ability to recognise such uptrends early in their development so as to benefit for as long as possible from the rise. The key to retaining such good profits is to be able to recognise when such a trend has ended so as to exit with a large proportion of the accumulated profit. The time of highest risk is when the share price is rapidly approaching the extrapolated trendline after falling back from one of the intermediate peaks. Since we have said that a slight tolerance is allowable, it is not correct to sell when the price touches the trendline, since during the time the uptrend has been in being, the share price has consistently bounced back up from it. The amount of penetration of the price down through the trendline which is allowable before the trend is considered to have been broken is then crucial. Most technical analysts settle for a 5% penetration of the trendline.

At the time of writing, the trendline is at a level of about 440p. Thus the price needs to fall below 418p for the trend to be considered to have come to an end. The price still has a further 40p to fall in a short time if this is to happen.

Note how profitable the rebounds from the trendline have been. In the case of the bounce in October 1988, the price rose to 440p, i.e. by virtually

100% in a very short time. The rise from the trough at 298p in May 1992 saw the price touch 500p within a few months. Thus investors following this trendline in BAT would have done exceedingly well over the past few years.

Note the major difference between a simple uptrend and a channelled uptrend: although the troughs all lie on a straight trendline, no such line can be drawn through the intermediate peaks so as to be parallel to the uptrend line. The peaks are at irregular heights above the rising trendline.

The chart of Marks and Spencer shown in Figure 8.2 is a wonderful example of the multiplicity of visits to the trendline that can occur. In this case there are now fewer than seven distinct and sharp troughs that lie either on it, or within one penny of it.

The chart is unusual in its behaviour once the line was penetrated on the downside. The price ran up to the peak value of 459.5p in January 1994, before gradually falling back. By 9th December 1994 the price had fallen to 369p, whereas the position of the trendline at that time was about 415p. Clearly the price was well below the 5% tolerance, so that the uptrend could be said to be broken. However, this low point of 369p was the lowest trough on a new uptrend line which was running virtually parallel to the first one. Not only that, but it could be argued that the new price movements are contained within a channel, the upper boundary of which is the

Figure 8.2 This medium term uptrend line in Marks and Spencer has seven troughs that lie on it. Once broken, a new uptrend line has been established

earlier trendline. In other words, what was a rising floor (i.e. support level) for the share price then became a rising ceiling (i.e. resistance level). As will be seen in the next chapter, this is a frequent occurrence with horizontal support and resistance lines.

As far as the new trendline is concerned, there have been three further troughs, in March 1995, November 1995 and March 1996, lying on this line, i.e. the new trendline has been in existence for over a year.

Hillsdown Holdings provides another example of a medium term uptrend, as shown in Figure 8.3. Starting in July 1993, the uptrend has four troughs lying on it.

Having peaked at 200p in August 1995, the line was penetrated on the downside in September 1995. At this time the line was at 177p, so that the 5% point below it was just over 168p. Following an initial bounce back to the level of the line, the price fell over the next few weeks until it dropped to 168p on 24th October. It continued downwards to the trough at 152p on 8th December. Thus from the point at which it fell below the line, the share price lost 14% of its value.

From this low point, the price rose again to 192p in March 1996 before falling to a trough at 166p. An interesting point is that if the two latest troughs are joined by a straight line, this line is parallel to the original trendline, but of course running at a lower level than the original.

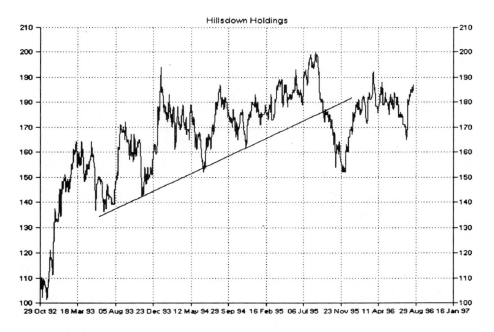

Figure 8.3 The uptrend in the Hillsdown Holdings share price ran for two years before falling in late 1995

Although, as stated before, two points do not constitute a trendline, we will yet see the same situation as in Marks and Spencer if the next fall takes the price to a trough which does lie on this new straight line.

Curved Uptrend

A curved uptrend differs from a straight uptrend by virtue of the fact that the troughs all lie on a curve. Although a curve can be drawn through any three troughs, a curved uptrend is much better defined if at least four troughs lie on it. The rule for deciding that the trend has come to an end is not quite the same as that for straight uptrends, since the curvature of the trendline plays an additional part.

A good example can be found in the price for RTZ between 1988 and 1990, as shown in Figure 8.4. The major troughs in December 1988, September 1989 and January 1990 all lie on a curved line whose curvature is decreasing. The trough in January 1990 lies on the best projection of the curve onwards from the trough in September 1989, and at this point the price would be watched very carefully for signs of falling significantly below the trendline. A major advantage of curved trendlines over straight ones is that there is another signal that the end of the trend is coming

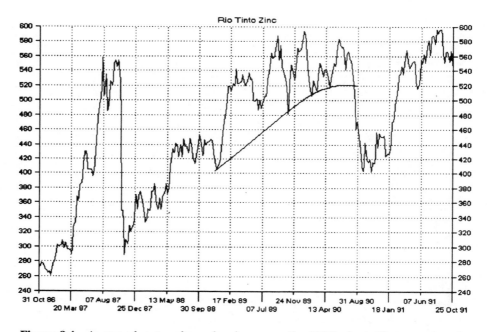

Figure 8.4 A curved uptrend can be drawn on the RTZ chart. The curvature is gradually decreasing, and the trend was broken in August 1990. The curve presents a concave aspect to the future

closer, and that is when the curve is flattening out. Thus in the present case, the next trough in April 1990 forced the curve to continue to flatten out, thus making the investor more aware that the next time the price fell back to the trendline could be the end of the trend. In July the price did fall back to a position slightly below the projected trendline at 521p and spent a few days hesitating at this level. Unlike the straight trendline, where the investor would still hang on because the price was not 5% below the trendline, a critical fact is that the price had fallen just a penny or so below that of the previous trough. This indicated that the curved trendline had passed its peak, and it was therefore time to sell. The price then collapsed rapidly to a level of just over 400p, justifying the selling decision.

The curvature of an uptrend can of course be in two forms. In the form shown in Figure 8.4 the curve presents a concave shape to future prices, whereas an alternative is one which presents a convex shape to the future. In an ideal world, whether a curve is convex or concave depends upon how far along a rising trend we happen to be when the prices conform to a curve. In the early stages of an uptrend the curve will be convex, whereas at a late stage it will be concave. A good example of a share which shows a curve changing from convex to concave as the uptrend develops is provided by the chart of GEC shown in Figure 8.5. Because of this change, the curve becomes chicane-shaped over the period from October 1991 to September 1993.

Figure 8.5 The GEC share price shows a curved uptrend in the form of a chicane. Thus the early part of the curve presents a convex aspect and the latter part a concave aspect to the future

Of the two types, concave and convex, the concave is the most useful in a predictive sense. This is because, since the curvature is getting less, it becomes obvious that the trend is running out of steam, and is therefore signalling quite clearly that the time is fast approaching when the investor should sell.

On the other hand, the convex curve can take the form either of the chicane, as shown in the GEC case, in which it has turned into a concave curve with its predictive advantages, or of an ever-increasing curvature which will come to a sudden end. In the latter case, the only judgement the investor can take is that the rate of climb has become unsustainable at some point in its development, and therefore the time has come to sell. The point at which it is judged to be unsustainable is therefore a very subjective one. An example of this is shown in the Tesco share price in Figure 8.6. The curved trend line is highly valid, since there are some eight troughs lying on it between September 1994 and August 1995. By the latter date the curve is rising almost vertically, and is obviously at a level which cannot be sustained. The price fell from a peak of 337.5p to 310p in the course of a few days, i.e. a loss of nearly 10%.

The best practice for an investor holding such a share when the curve becomes nearly vertical is to decide to get out on any fall, i.e. ignore the

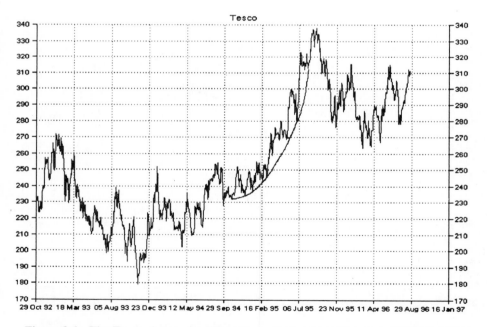

Figure 8.6 The Tesco share price. Here the curved uptrend is convex with respect to the future. It has reached an unsustainable rate of increase from which the price falls rapidly. There are eight troughs lying on the line

stop loss method, since the price more often than not will fall in a similar way to that of Tesco. By this method, the investor would have got out at about 327p, only about 3% down from the peak, rather than having to accept a loss of around 10%.

Note the all-important difference between a curved uptrend and a channel. It is not possible to draw a curve through the peaks in these examples such that the gap between them remains constant, since they are at irregular price levels. For a channelled uptrend, this will be possible.

Straight Downtrend

As mentioned earlier in this book, downtrend lines are constructed by drawing a straight line through three or more peaks. The chart of Safeway shown in Figure 8.7 is a good example of a downtrend changing into a curved uptrend. The downtrend lasted for most of 1988, and the trendline can be seen to have begun with the peak of 210p on 18th March 1988. The peaks between this point and the peak in July at 194p would have resulted in a trendline being drawn with a greater downwards slope than that shown in the figure, but the peak in July would force a slight adjustment. The price fell away again and it was another three months before the same trendline was picked up again. The next peak on 29th October at 180p was

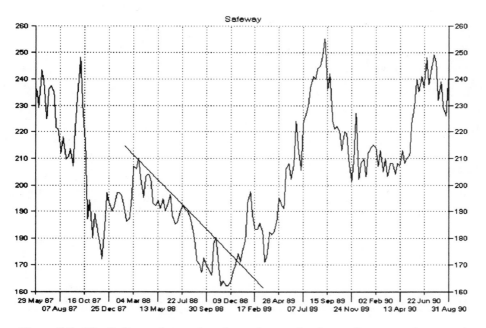

Figure 8.7 The Safeway share price. A good example of a medium term downtrend that lasted just under a year

the fifth point lying on or very close to the line, giving a well-defined trend. The investor would now be looking for a rise of 5% above this line. The price fell away considerably from this peak to a low point of 162p on 11th November 1988 and then rose sharply to a level of 179p to penetrate the line. This represents just over 5% above the trendline itself, and in view of the strength of the line with four peaks on it and one peak close to it, can be considered to be an unambiguous signal that the downtrend has been broken. The correctness of this view is supported by the fact that the price rose rapidly to 197.5p on 3rd February. The low point of 11th November was a major low, being the lowest point reached in the last five years.

By March 1989 the price retreated to the first of a series of troughs which formed a new major uptrend which took the price up to an all-time high in August 1989.

Note the all-important difference between a downtrend and a down-channel. It is not possible to draw a straight line through the troughs, since they are at irregular price levels. For a downchannel, as will be seen shortly, it is possible to draw another line through the troughs which is parallel to the line through the peaks.

Some downtrends last a very long time, as can be seen from the example of George Wimpey, shown in Figure 8.8. The trend can be considered to have started with the peak on 17th February 1989, with the price at 307p.

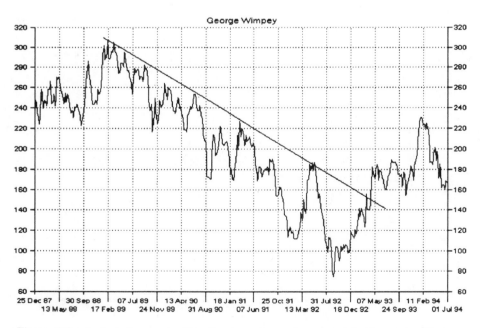

Figure 8.8 A first-class example of a long term downtrend is shown by George Wimpey. The trend lasted over five years, from February 1989 until April 1993

The next peak, just a few weeks later, was at 305p. The fact that this peak was lower than the previous one is an indication that the previous uptrend may have changed direction. The next peak in May 1989 was still lower, at 295p, and at this point it was possible to draw a trendline sloping downwards.

The trendline would have to be adjusted slightly when the next peak was formed at 282p on 8th September 1989, but the previous peaks would have been well within the tolerance permissible.

It was a further nine months before the price rose to this line again with the peak at 253p on 22nd June 1990. Following a further attempt at crossing the line in March 1991, the price spent a long time below the line before a return in May 1992. As will be discussed in the next chapter, this peak was composed of a number of extremely short term small peaks, giving the appearance of a flag. This usually means a further rise, but in this case the trendline obviously carried more weight in deciding the future price movement than the flag, since the price then retreated down to a low of 74p, the lowest price for more than a decade.

The rise from this level took the price up to the trendline once more, and reached it on 19th March 1993 at 155p, before bouncing down again. Thus the trendline is still seen to have had an influence even though the end of the actual downtrend can be considered to have been reached with the low of 74p.

A few weeks later, the price decisively penetrated the trendline with a rise to 182p on 23rd April 1993. Note that an investor selling the share at that time would have seen a 25% rise to 228p by early 1994, before the price fell back to the 160p level.

The downtrend shown in the chart of Hillsdown in Figure 8.9 lasted just over three years. An unusual feature is the sharpness of the first three peaks which touch the trendline. In each case the price jumped by about 10p in a day to take it to the trendline, as if the trendline were exerting its influence to provide a final spurt to the price even as the price was already hesitating before beginning its downward journey once more.

Curved Downtrend

Just as there are curved versions of uptrends, so can we find curved versions of downtrends. As with uptrends, there are two versions of the curve—those which present a concave face to the future, and those which are convex with respect to the future. An example of a concave curved downtrend is shown for Coats Viyella in Figure 8.10.

The curve is drawn through six peaks in the price, and unlike most curves is almost exactly an arc of a circle, i.e. its curvature remains constant throughout its length. At the time of writing the price is at its furthest excursion from the trend, being some 45p below the point at which the curved trend is about to turn up. Thus it is possible that the

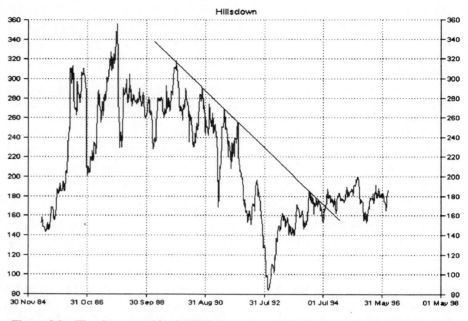

Figure 8.9   The downtrend in the Hillsdown share price has needlepoint peaks touching it

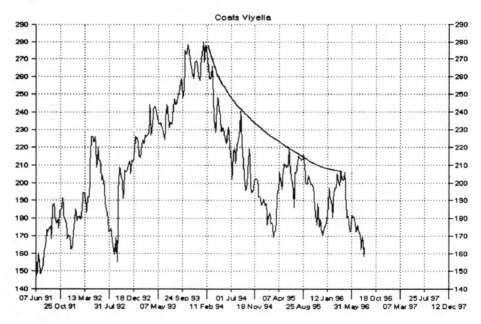

Figure 8.10   A curved downtrend lasting over two years can be seen in the Coats Viyella share price. The curve is concave with respect to the future

curve represents the first half of a rounded bottom where the short term fluctuations are much greater than in a traditional rounded bottom as discussed in the last chapter. In this particular example, the value of the trend lies in its projection following the peak in August 1995. Because of the constant radius of the curve, its projection is quite easy to draw. Thus the arrival of the price in March and April 1996 at the projection would have sounded a warning bell to the investor holding the share that the time had come to sell. The resulting 45p fall shows how valid the warning was.

Convex curved downtrends are not quite as common, but a short term example is shown in Figure 8.11 for British Gas. The first peak on the downtrend is at 276p on 5th September 1995. A curve could not be drawn until the third peak at 265.5p on 4th October. At this point the price fell away sharply to 245p in a matter of days, but bounced back again to meet the extrapolated curve on 18th October at 260.5p. As with the previous example, the curvature of the curve remains constant, i.e. it maintains a constant radius from its centre, so that extrapolation is easy. As before, the price reacted markedly, falling from this point to below 230p. It can be seen that each reaction from the curve is progressively greater.

The price rose again from this low point to reach the curve for the fifth time at a price of 245.5p on 14th November. Although the price fell again, on this occasion the reaction was slight, and the price came back to a

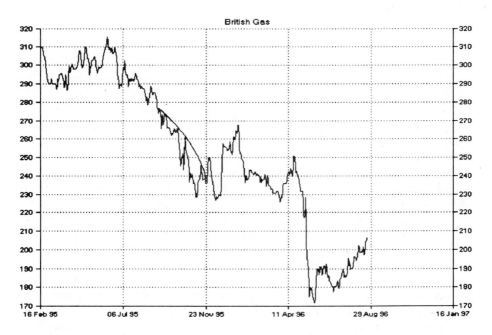

Figure 8.11 A short term curved downtrend in British Gas. This curve is convex with respect to the future

minor peak of 238.5p on 21st November. This peak is again on the extrapolated curve, but the reaction this time was so minor that the expectation
was that the downtrend would be violated quite soon.

At this point the extrapolated curve is falling nearly vertically, so that it
must be at an end. The price rapidly rose to 250p before falling once more,
but from this fall a rapid rise occurred to 257.5p on 21st December 1995.
Thus the investor correctly identifying the end of the trend from the
vertical fall of the curve and the progressively smaller reactions from the
curve would have made a useful profit in a very short time.

CHANNELLED TRENDS

Channelled trends are uptrends and downtrends in which the excursions
away from the trendline are limited by another line which is at a constant
vertical distance from the trendline. In the case of an uptrend, this second
line will be above it, whereas with downtrends, it will be below it. These
two lines can be considered to be boundaries, within which the price is
contained for the duration of their existence, whereas in the uptrends and
downtrends discussed earlier, the excursions were not limited, so that the
trends appeared to be somewhat irregular. As with simple trends, channelled trends can be straight or curved.

Straight Upchannel

Scottish and Newcastle provides an excellent example (Figure 8.12) of a
straight upchannel. As shown in the figure, a straight trendline can be
drawn so as to touch exactly the troughs that occurred in March 1995,
November 1995, December 1995 and March 1996. Although in this example the troughs fall exactly on a straight line, in practice a small amount
of tolerance can be accepted, so that the price may bounce up just before a
trendline is reached, or pass a small distance below the line before the
price rises once again.

The upper boundary which limits movement away from the trendline is
at a vertical distance of about 60p above it. It passes through the tips of the
group of peaks between July 1995 and September 1995, but is not revisited
until the peak in April 1996. Thus the channel lasted about a year.

On 21st June 1996, the lower boundary was at a level of 670p. The price
fell below this before recovering slightly. This time the recovery took the
price up to what was previously the lower boundary before reacting downwards again. Thus, what was the lower boundary has now become an
upper boundary, preventing the price moving higher.

The price fell to below 640p before climbing again, but the latest peak is
at a similar level to the previous one at 670p. Thus it has to be considered
that the uptrend is now at an end.

Figure 8.12 A straight upchannel in the Scottish and Newcastle Breweries share price

It is important that unlike the case with simple uptrends, investors do not use the fall of 5% below the lower boundary as a selling signal. Many channels are of large depth, so that the fall when a share price peaks at the upper boundary and drops to the lower boundary can be large. The only way in which penetration of the lower boundary of a channelled uptrend should be used is as an indication that the price is now headed on a downtrend, of indeterminate length. As will be seen in the chapter on Channel Analysis, a close study of the behaviour of price movement within channels can be extremely rewarding in terms of much sharper timing of buying and selling points.

Note that on the visits to the lower boundary, the price rebounded about 10% each time in the space of just a few days, giving a very respectable short term profit for the investor who bought at those points.

In the case of Charter Consolidated (Figure 8.13), the straight upchannel has lasted for nearly three years, and at the time of writing is not yet at an end. The lower boundary has five troughs lying on it, starting with two fairly close together in mid-1992. It was July 1994 before the next trough was formed on the lower boundary, but meanwhile there had been two peaks formed, in January 1993 and January 1994. The straight line joining these two peaks would be parallel to an extension of the line joining the two troughs in 1992, and therefore it can be considered by the time of this second peak that we probably have a channelled uptrend developing. The fact that the trough in 1994 falls on the extension of the lower line is confirmation of this fact. Thus the rebound of this price from the trough in July 1994 is a signal to buy. The extension of the upper boundary gives an idea of the extent of the price rise which should ensue. Since the vertical depth of the channel is now about 180p, we would have to take this amount and add to it the amount by which the channel has risen from the trough by the time the price reaches the upper boundary. However, since this is an indeterminate amount, our best guess is a rise of at least 180p. As can be seen from the chart, the price rose from this trough of 663p on 27th June 1994 to 835p on 29th August 1994, a rise of 172p. The investor of course would not have got into the share at the trough of 663p, but a few days later at about 670p once the trough had been formed. The investor would have been pleased with the subsequent gain of nearly 25%.

Curved Upchannel

Curved channelled trends are equally as common as straight ones, and the chart of Ladbroke in Figure 8.14 shows such a curved uptrend running over most of 1988. A lower boundary can be drawn through five troughs, starting with the trough immediately after the fall in October 1987 and ending with the trough in December 1988. A curved upper boundary can

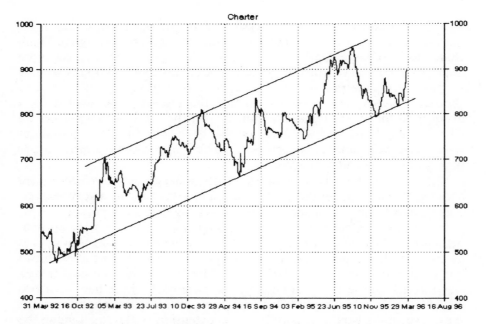

Figure 8.13   The Charter Consolidated share price shows a long term straight upchannel which has lasted for nearly four years

also be drawn to cover the same time period and passing through the peaks in March 1988, July 1988 and September 1988. By the end of 1988 the curve was quite obviously flattening out, and therefore the investor would be expecting the end of the uptrend to be signalled by a breakout through the lower boundary. Perversely the breakout was through the upper boundary in January 1989. What this means is that the short term uptrend was replaced by a much stronger longer term uptrend, which took the share price up much more rapidly. The price eventually peaked out at around 340p before a series of short term cycles came into prominence which were superimposed on the stronger uptrend which was now topping out. The channel presents a concave face to the future.

An example of a channel with a convex face to the future can be seen in Figure 8.15. Here the GKN share price is contained within a channel which is increasing in slope, and obviously building to a rate of increase that cannot be sustained. Although the channel appears to be getting narrower, this is an illusion, since the vertical depth is constant, a feature which is mandatory for all curved channels.

A closer inspection shows that the price penetrated through the lower boundary once it bounced back for the second time from the 1000p resistance level, so that the rising channel must now be considered to be at an end.

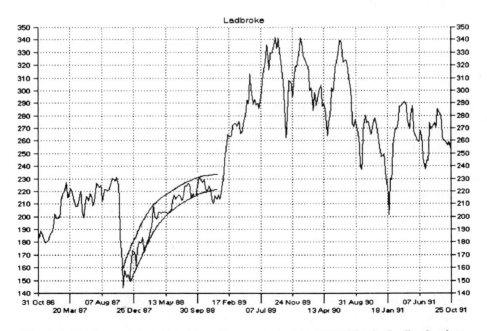

Figure 8.14 A curved upchannel can be seen over most of 1988 in the Ladbroke share price

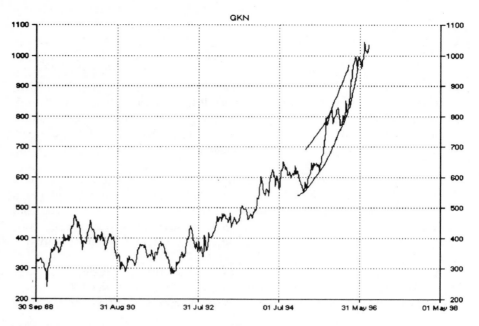

Figure 8.15 The GKN price is contained in a channel which is convex with respect to the future. The channel curvature is such that the upward trend is unsustainable

An investor who got into the share at the beginning of the upwards channel movement would have seen a rise in price from about 550p to 1000p in just over a year, a rise of 81%.

Straight Downchannel

A well-defined short term channelled downtrend is shown in Figure 8.16 for BTR. The upper boundary has five peaks either on it or within a penny of it. The lower boundary has three troughs lying on it, but it is exactly parallel to the upper boundary of the channel. The usual breakout from a descending channelled trend is of course on the upper side, i.e. the downtrend turns into an uptrend. In this case, however, the price penetrated the lower boundary to fall away drastically from 312p to 238p in a matter of a month.

Although naturally a stop loss would prevent such an excessive loss, the penetration of a channel on either boundary is a warning that the trend is changing direction.

A much longer channelled downtrend is exhibited by Glynwed (Figure 8.17). The trend started with the market crash in October 1987, prior to which the share price reached a peak of 384p. The trough into which the price then fell was at 258p, 126p lower. Since this fall was almost vertical, it gives us a channel depth of just under 126p which was only broken in early

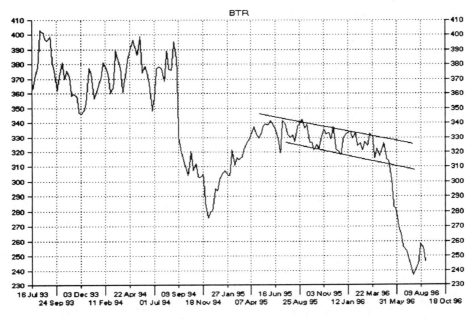

Figure 8.16 A short term channelled downtrend in the BTR share price

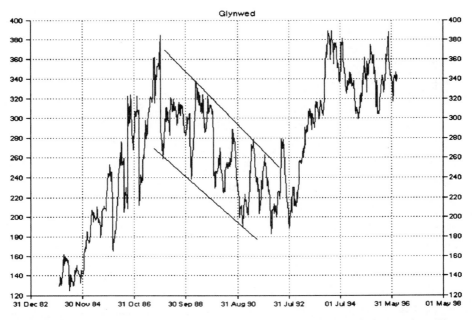

Figure 8.17 A long term channelled downtrend in the Glynwed share price. The trend lasted nearly five years

1992. It should be noted that the previous history of Glynwed was one of rapid rises and falls of the order of 100p to 120p, so that the fall occasioned by the crash was not unusual as far as this share was concerned. The movement subsequent to the crash was equally erratic, so that the price swung repeatedly between the channel boundaries.

The trend was broken in April 1992 when the price rose above 218p to 280p, this peak being well above the upper boundary. This move was not decisive, since the price immediately fell back into the channel again, but this time did no more than meet the mid-point at 188p on 7th August before rising again. This time the rise was sustained and took the price back to the levels reached just prior to the 1987 crash.

The investor taking advantage of the share pushing up through the upper boundary would still have made a small profit from the first, temporary penetration, with a rise from 247p to 280p, but obviously the real profit was made on the second occasion with a rise from 241p (the boundary position) to 388p.

Curved Downchannel

Enterprise Oil, shown in Figure 8.18, is a good example of a curved downtrend. In this case the curve is concave with respect to the future. The

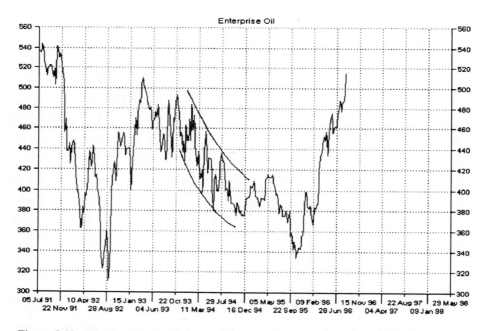

Figure 8.18   The Enterprise Oil share price is contained in a channel which is concave with respect to the future. The channel curvature is such that the downward trend appears to be approaching its end

channel depth is about 65p, and the short term oscillations within the channel almost go from boundary to boundary within a few days, rises and falls of about 60p being the norm.

By the end of 1994, the channel curvature is rapidly flattening out, so that the expectation is that the long term price trend should change direction soon. In May 1995, the price broke up through the upper boundary, but this was a false signal, since the price then fell down through the upper boundary and then down through the lower boundary. The downward trend finally changed direction in November 1995 when the price rose from the trough of 337p. The share made substantial progress over the next nine months.

Coats Viyella, shown in Figure 8.19, is interesting because of the existence of two curved downchannels, a short term one and a medium term one. These are of opposite curvature. The first of these, the short term concave channel, can be seen from late 1987 to mid-1988. It is very well defined, having four troughs lying on the lower boundary, and five peaks lying on the upper boundary. This is one of those cases where it is essential to wait for a break through a boundary before taking any investment decision. Quite obviously, the channel is a curve that is flattening out, and so there is every indication that the price should start to rise again. Those

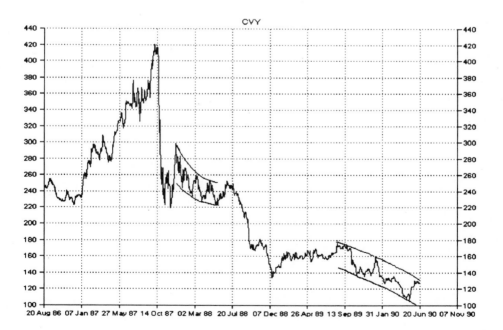

Figure 8.19 The Coats Viyella price contains two curved downchannels of opposite curvature. The first, following the market crash of 1987, is concave while the second is convex

investors who by their nature have a tendency to jump the gun would come to grief, because they would be totally convinced that once the price had reached the bottom of the channel in August 1988 the only way it could go would be upwards. As will be seen from the chapter on channel analysis, such premature action is never to be taken, and confirmation that a channel has passed its bottom point must be seen before action is taken. In the case of Coats Viyella, the investor would see that there is no bounce back from the bottom of the channel, and the price fell down through it. The conclusion, therefore, is that the gradually straightening downtrend has been replaced by a much more severe downtrend, and no investment would have been made at that point.

Once the share price had climbed back slightly from the trough in December 1988, the share entered a new channelled trend which again was curving downwards, but presenting a convex shape to the future. This channel has some four peaks touching the upper boundary, two of which occurred very close together. The lower boundary has three troughs lying on it. With the price at the upper boundary the investor would be looking quite closely for signs of penetration upwards. The probability is against this because the downtrend is in an early stage of its development, having increased its curvature only slightly over the period of the trend.

9

Hesitation Patterns

The patterns which will be discussed here are often gathered together under the term 'continuation patterns', but this is a misnomer, since many of the patterns are in an ambiguous state where they can continue the previous trend or reverse it. A much better term is that used for the title of this chapter, 'hesitation patterns', since the term is then self-explanatory. The share price is in a phase in which it is making up its mind about its future direction, and the future direction is not known until a breakout from the pattern occurs. Except for the special case of flags, these patterns can be of medium or short term. Flag patterns are periods of hesitation which last for up to a few weeks, usually taken to be about three weeks maximum, and are therefore special cases of these more general hesitation patterns.

SUPPORT/RESISTANCE LINES

Support lines are horizontal lines from which the share price repeatedly bounces back upwards. Resistance lines are lines from which the share price repeatedly bounces back downwards. The reason for bracketing these two together in this heading is that it very often happens that once a resistance line is violated, it then becomes a support line, and once a support line is violated it then becomes a resistance line.

While two or three troughs can fall to exactly the same value and two or three peaks rise to the same value, giving an exactly horizontal support or resistance line, it is unusual for many more troughs or peaks to fall exactly on the line. For these extended cases a small amount of tolerance is to be expected, but this should be no more than 2–3% of the level of the line in question. This is exemplified by the share price of Land Securities (Figure 9.1) through most of 1988 and 1989. There is obviously a line of resistance at about 600p above which the share price has failed to move despite numerous attempts during this period of time. The first peak at the start of this resistance was on 20th May 1988 at 596p. The price fell back slightly before having another go at this level a few weeks later, this time advancing slightly to 598p on 15th June. It was another five months before a third attempt was made on this level, and this time the price broke through to 609p on 23rd November. Since this is only 2% above the first of these attempts, it cannot be considered that the line has been broken, and this was confirmed by the fact that the price then fell back once again. A new attempt was made in February 1989 which took the price up to a peak of 600p, but again this failed to make a decisive breakthrough. Several further efforts in March and May took the price to 593p and 596p before the price rose to 609p on 12th April 1989. By this time the view would have been formed that the real resistance line was at 600p, and that the very small penetrations were simply a random fluctuation about this line. Thus a rise to 609p represents a rise of only 1.5% through this line, and cannot be considered to be significant. Sure enough, the price fell back again before reaching the 600p level again on 17th August. Finally the price struggled to 605p on 5th September 1989 before giving up and falling away rapidly to below 500p, and then further in the next two years to 358p in September 1992.

Thus the history of the Land Securities share price was one of numerous attempts to cross the 600p level decisively and of constant failure to do this. Since a resistance line may be considered to be a horizontal trendline, we have to adopt the same criterion for penetration as we did with

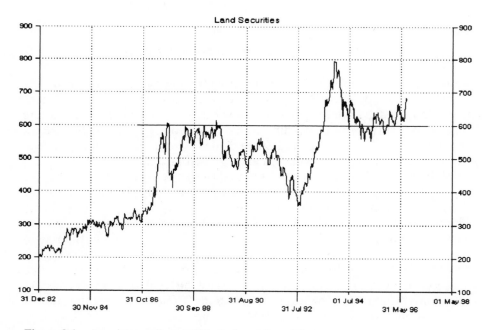

Figure 9.1   A resistance line at 600p in Land Securities

trendlines: the price has to penetrate the resistance line by 5% before we can consider that the resistance has been broken.

It was nearly four years before the Land Securities price got back to the level of the resistance line, and the price crossed it decisively on this occasion, rising from 608p on 23rd July 1993 to a peak of just under 800p. In falling back from this point, the 600p level became a temporary support line, with the price bouncing upwards from it. It then became a temporary resistance line, before becoming a support line once more. Thus the 600p level in Land Securities is an important interface between low price levels and high price levels.

An example where there were fewer attempts to cross a resistance line, but where the line still stayed valid for almost two years, can be seen in Reed International (Figure 9.2). Nearly one year after the October 1987 crash the price had recovered about half of the lost ground, rising to a peak of 468p on 1st August 1988. The price then fell back before rising again to a peak of 460p on 8th February 1989. Again the share price failed to make any further progress and fell to its low for the year in December. Following a fall back in the beginning of 1989, the price then recovered gradually before peaking out at 467p on 24th August. We can now see that since this is within a penny of the peak back in August 1988 we can construct a resistance line at this level, even though 467p or 468p seems to be an odd level for resistance. The line was validated by another attempt

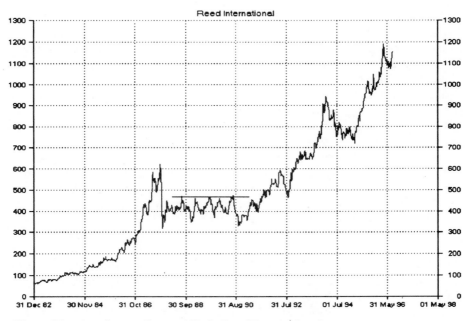

Figure 9.2 A resistance line at 467p in Reed International

at this level on 28th June 1990, when the price peaked at 467p again. Although the price broke through this line to 472p a few weeks later on 19th July, this is only 1% above the line, and nothing like the 5% break-through that is required to substantiate a failure of the resistance. The price rose back to the resistance line again in August 1991, before crossing it and the 500p line in September 1991. Although the rise from that point to 600p was of only short duration, the price eventually left this congested area for the last time in August 1992 with the low at 460p. Since then the share has risen to over twice this level.

The same philosophy of allowing a little tolerance either side of a support or resistance line can be seen in the case of Blue Circle Industries (Figure 9.3). Following a sharp recovery from the crash of 1987, the share price then fell back to 202p on 12th February 1988 before apparently resuming its upwards move. It was three months before the price fell back again, drop-ping to 203p on 29th April and staying at that general level until the price inched down to 201p on 27th May 1988. Another three months later the price was back down to 204p on 2nd September, but then made some progress before running out of steam again and moving back down to 203p on 23rd December. This time the price moved upwards consistently, and by the following May was at a peak of 292p. The price then spent the next five months falling back to the resistance level, reaching 196p on 27th October 1989. A rally took the price up again before it dropped back once more. This time the price fell very slightly through the previously established resistance line, reaching 202p on 4th May before recovering again. Taking all of the trough prices into account, the resistance line is best drawn at 205p, so as to put all of the troughs into the position of being randomly and, importantly, closely scattered about it. The 5% breakthrough line can there-fore be drawn at 195p. The price fell below this line to 189p on 17th July 1992. Once this support was left behind, a substantial fall occurred, with the price bottoming out in October 1992 at 131p. The rise from this point was rapid, and the support line did not turn out to be a resistance line, since the price went rapidly through it. The next 18 months saw a rise to a sharp peak at 382.5p in January 1994.

So far, we have been looking at quite long term support and resistance lines, and the majority fall into this category. Sometimes, however, support or resistance can last for just a few weeks. An example is shown in Figure 9.4 for Cable & Wireless. The resistance line shown at 462p lasted for just two months in 1996. The line was touched by the peak on 4th January 1996, and again on 22nd January. The price then fell to a trough of 432.5 on 29th January before it rose slightly above the line at 463p. The last touch with the line was on 21st February. A few weeks later the price rose through the resistance line to 477p on 11th March, before making a large jump to 538p.

It frequently happens that a line can be both a resistance line and a support line, changing from one to the other once the price penetrates

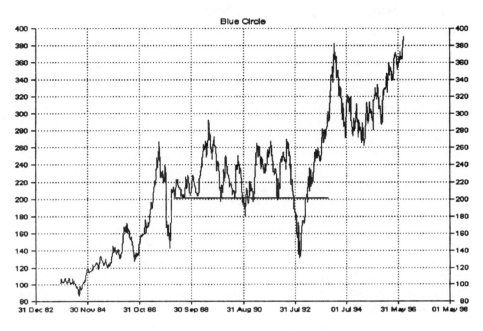

Figure 9.3   More tolerance is needed to draw the Blue Circle resistance line

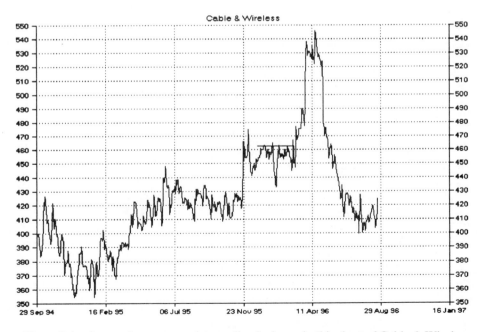

Figure 9.4   A very short term resistance line is shown in this chart of Cable & Wireless

through. A good example of this is Allied Domecq, shown in Figure 9.5. The line in question is one that can be drawn at the level of 550p. This particular section of the share price features multiple short term price movements that take the price up and down in rapid jumps or falls of over 100p. The first trough on or near the resistance line was in September 1992 at 550p, the next in April 1993 at 551p, following which the price fell temporarily below the line to a trough at 523p in May 1993. The price then recovered to the territory above the line, forming more troughs on the line in November 1993, April 1994 and July 1994. The price then fell rapidly to 498p before rising to the line, which now became a resistance level, with peaks in July 1995, August 1995 and January 1996. Having failed to penetrate the resistance line, the price fell by over 100p in the course of the next few months, and at the time of writing is still around the 450p mark.

From these few examples, it can be seen that support and resistance lines can be valid for anything from a few weeks to many years. In general, once the price has crossed the line, there is usually a rapid movement away from the line, with large falls from a support line, and large rises from a resistance line. More often than not, the line then changes character from being a support line to a resistance line and vice versa.

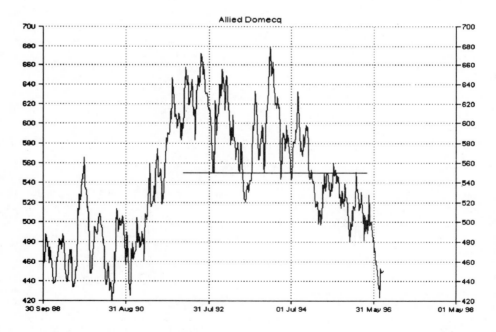

Figure 9.5 A resistance line can become a support line as shown by the line at 552p in Allied Domecq

RECTANGLES

A rectangle is an area of congestion of the share price that is limited by
both a support line and a resistance line, so that the price spends its time
oscillating between the two levels. Since the two lines are parallel to each
other, the formation is known as a rectangle. As with normal support and
resistance lines, a certain tolerance should be allowed for crossing of these
lines, but a 5% crossing is taken to be significant for a continued move in
the direction of the penetration.

A medium term rectangle can be seen in Figure 9.6 for Glaxo Holdings.
The rectangle can be said to have started in June 1989 with the price at a
trough of 337p. The price then spent the next year between the extremes
of 337p and 405p, and only moved outside this range at the end of 1990. As
with resistance lines, once this had been crossed, the price rose dramatically to over 900p, i.e. more than double the level of the resistance line in
less than a year.

It is not possible to predict whether the price will break upwards or
downwards from the congested area of a rectangle formation. It will only
be possible to say at the time that it happens that a new trend is in
progress. As with the rise above the resistance line in the case of Glaxo, a
fall below the support line would be expected to produce a considerable
price fall.

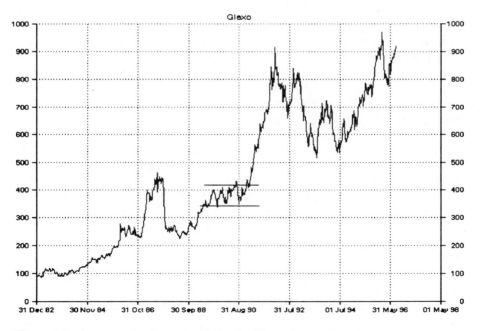

Figure 9.6   An example of a rectangle in the Glaxo share price

TRIANGLES

There are many forms of triangles, the main types of which are discussed in this section. Since these formations are so common, it is not necessary to provide more than one example of each type. The crucial aspect of triangles is that a break-out through a side is significant, implying further movement in the same direction, while for triangles other than expanders, there is no significance if the price meanders through to the point. In such a case the future direction of the price cannot be predicted. More often than not, a break-out from a triangle is such that the trend prior to the triangle formation continues, but there are so many examples of opposite behaviour that an investor must wait for the break-out to occur before taking a position.

Since the side of a triangle through which the price breaks out can also be considered to be a trendline, the same criterion must be applied as with trendlines, viz. that a 5% penetration must occur before the penetration is seen as significant. This is true whether a horizontal or sloping side is being considered.

Note that it is extremely rare to be able to construct a triangle in which all peaks exactly touch one side and all troughs exactly touch the opposite side. A degree of tolerance must be allowed.

Expanding Triangles

Although in theory expanding triangles should be no less common than contracting ones, in practice they are quite rare. They take the form of a cyclic oscillation in the share price growing in amplitude as time goes by. Since they are quite rare, it is not necessary to subdivide them into further categories of right-angles, isosceles, etc. These expanding triangles are imperfect in the sense that they do not start from a point, but the first oscillation within their confines is normally quite small. An excellent example of an expander where a break-out in either direction has yet to occur can be found in the Pearson share price, as shown in Figure 9.7. The first peak that can be identified as lying on the upper side of the triangle is in June 1995, followed by a trough in early July. The next peak on the upper side of the triangle was in August 1995. Subsequent troughs all lie on a horizontal line, defining the lower side of the triangle. However, the peaks lie on or close to the line which was drawn through the first two peaks, so defining the upper side of the triangle. The price is still contained within the triangle. The most probable break-out from this formation is through the lower line, which of course is a resistance line by the criteria discussed earlier. Once the price breaks out the usual fall to be predicted is for a similar distance below the lower side of the triangle as the length of the third side, i.e. the distance between the upper and lower sides at the time of penetration.

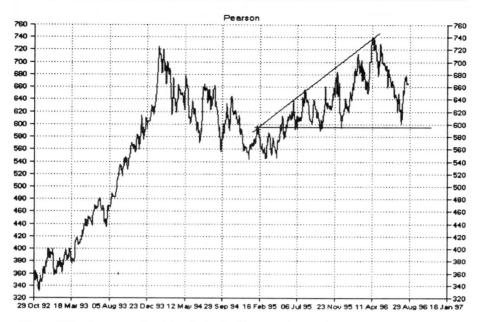

Pearson

Figure 9.7 An expanding triangle in the Pearson share price

Ascending Right-angled Triangle

The upper side of these triangles is horizontal, and can therefore be considered to be a resistance line. The lower side is sloping upwards, i.e. ascending, and can be considered to be a rising trendline which acts as a support line. The two lines meet at the apex of the triangle. The price movement is contained between these two lines because short term oscillations are gradually reducing in importance.

A good example here is the case of Thames Water in late 1994 and early 1995 (Figure 9.8). There are some five peaks which form the upper, horizontal side of the triangle at a level of about 493p, and four troughs which lie on or close to the ascending line shown.

Since the horizontal line is at 493p, the 5% level is 518p, i.e. a rise above this level is necessary in order to be significant. Thus the short term rise to 514p does not meet this 5% criterion, so that no investment action would be taken on this rise. The same applies to the fall below the ascending side of the triangle, and so the sharp fall to 472p is some 4p above the threshold required. Although the price exits from the triangle fairly near the apex, it is not exactly at the apex, and therefore the above comment predicting the subsequent price movement does not apply. Here the exit from the upper side implies a further rise, a prediction which can be seen to be true.

A triangle occurring over a much shorter time span can be seen in the case of Zeneca (Figure 9.9). The triangle covers just five months, and as

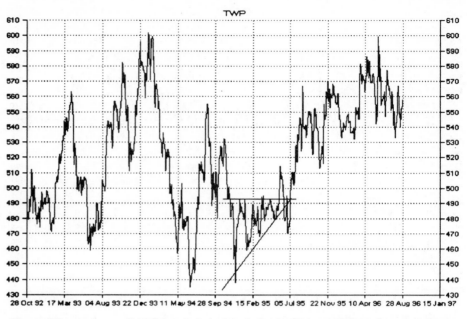

Figure 9.8 An ascending right-angled triangle in the Thames Water share price

Figure 9.9 A short term ascending right-angled triangle in the Zeneca share price.
Following a temporary break-out through the top, the price has broken out upwards
near the apex

with the previous example there is a false break-out on the upper side of
the triangle which does not achieve the 5% threshold. A few weeks later
the price does rise by more than the 5% level to just over 1500p, although
it remains to be seen how significant the break-out will be over the course
of the next few months.

Descending Right-angled Triangle

The lower side of these triangles is horizontal, and can therefore be considered to be a support line. The upper side is sloping downwards, i.e.
descending, and can be considered to be a falling trendline which acts as a
resistance line. The two lines meet at the apex of the triangle. The price
movement is contained between these two lines because short term oscillations are gradually reducing in importance.

A medium term descending triangle can be seen in the Reed International share price during 1994 (Figure 9.10). The oscillations in the price
are at their maximum of about 220p at the beginning of the triangle in late
November 1993. The price rose from 727p in November to 947p by 31st
January 1994. The oscillations gradually died down to just a few pence
before the price left the triangle virtually at its apex in March 1995.

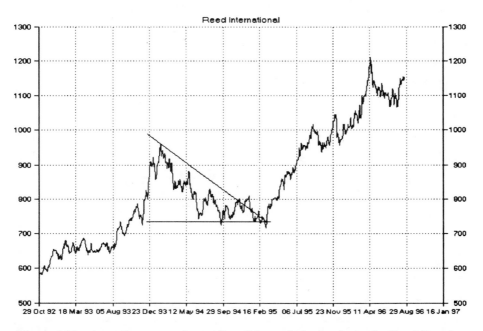

Figure 9.10 A medium term descending right-angled triangle in the Reed International share price. Since the price left the triangle at its apex, it was not possible to
predict the future direction of the price movement

Because the price leaves the triangle at this point, rather than by breaking through one of the sides, the future course of the price cannot be predicted until a 5% movement has occurred in a particular direction. In this example the price rose consistently over the following year.

An example of a descending triangle where the price left well before the apex can be seen in the Adwest share price (Figure 9.11). The base of the triangle can be seen to run at around 152p. The price entered the triangle in April 1993 and rose to 198p before falling back to the base. The next peak at 202p was the first peak on the upper side of the triangle. The price oscillations gradually dampened as time progressed, and the price dropped through the base in September 1995. The significance level 5% below the triangle base at 152p lies at 143p, and the price dropped below this to 142p on 27th October. This heralded a significant fall from that point onwards, the price reaching 112p by 11th March 1996.

A two-year triangle can be seen in the chart of the FTSE100 Index (Figure 9.12). The price entered it on 6th January 1993 and finally left it in March 1995. The first peak was at 3520.3 in February 1994, and the next trough was in June 1994 at 2931.9. The initial oscillation of more than 500 points was gradually whittled down to 100-point fluctuations by the end of 1994 and the beginning of 1995. In contrast to the previous example, the price left the triangle on the upper side. This break-out was significant, since the Index then rose consistently to the 3800 level.

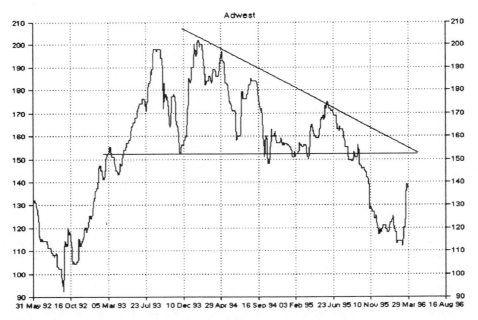

Figure 9.11 A descending right-angled triangle in Adwest is followed by a significant break-out through the base of the triangle

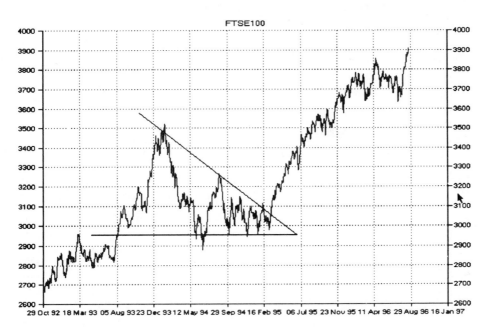

Figure 9.12 A long term descending triangle in the FTSE100 Index in which the break-out is through the upper side

These two examples where breakouts have occurred on opposite sides of the triangle show how important it is to wait for the 5% significance level to be broken before any investment action is taken.

Isosceles Triangle

A good example of an isosceles triangle can be found in the National Power share price during the second half of 1994 and the first half of 1995 (Figure 9.13). The line drawn through the tops of the succession of peaks formed during this period slopes downwards, while the line joining the troughs slopes upwards. Thus we have a rising uptrend acting as a support line, and a falling downtrend acting as a resistance line. The slopes of these lines are such that the triangle formed is virtually symmetrical about a horizontal line drawn through the apex, i.e. is isosceles. Because a horizontal line in the previous two types of triangle is replaced by a sloping line in this case, this necessarily means that the amplitude of the short term oscillations is being reduced much more rapidly than in the previous cases.

This example is characterised by a false break-out from the lower side of the triangle. At the time the price fell below the lower side, the triangle side was at 470p. Thus the 5% point would lie at 446.5p. The price dropped below this, but the fall thereafter was modest, reaching 426p. However, the

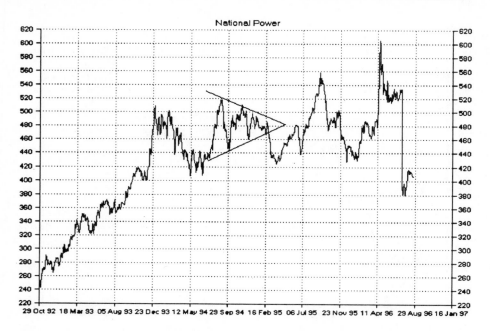

Figure 9.13 An isosceles triangle in National Power. The price break-out through the lower side was quickly reversed into a price rise

investor selling at 445p would be reasonably pleased when the price continued down a further 20p or so without him. However, he would have been less pleased with the subsequent movement, since from this point the price rose to the level of the apex of the triangle at 480p before reacting back to 439p and then reaching a high of 558p.

Scalene Triangle (Wedge)

So far we have looked at two types of triangle, those with upper and lower sides sloping in opposite directions and those with one side horizontal and one side sloping either down or up. There is obviously a third type in which both sides slope in the same direction, but at different angles. These are known as wedges, and of course they can point either upwards or downwards.

We saw that triangles in which the short term oscillations were increasing, i.e. the triangle was expanding, were very rare, but triangles in which the short term oscillations were decreasing were common. The same is true of wedges. The vast majority are those in which the oscillations are decreasing, so that the wedge points to the future. Logically, there should be no reason why a reverse-pointing wedge should not occur, but they are very uncommon.

Figure 9.14   An expanding wedge formation in the British Steel share price

Expanding Wedge

One of the few examples to be found is shown in Figure 9.14. The price is contained between two lines that are rising, with the amplitude of the short term oscillations increasing. At the time of writing the future direction of the price is yet to be determined, since the price has not penetrated either of the two containing lines.

The difference in slope of the two lines is not great, which accounts for the fact that the point of the wedge is well in the past, before 30th December 1988 at which the timescale of the chart begins.

The base of the wedge has five troughs lying close to or on it, starting with the one in December 1993 and ending with the one in July 1996. There are five peaks lying close to or on the upper side, the last one being in April 1996.

Contracting Wedge

The vast majority of wedges have their points directed to the future, due to the fact that the lower of the two lines forming the wedge has a lesser slope than the upper because of the reducing nature of the short term oscillations contained between the two lines.

Some writers maintain that the more usual break-out from a wedge formation is in the opposite direction to the way the wedge is pointing, but in this author's experience the break-out is more often such as to reverse the direction of the trend entering the pattern. There are several examples of wedges in the top 100 shares over the last few years, and they nearly all follow this rule.

A good long term example is that of United Biscuits, shown in Figure 9.15. The trend at the point of entry into the wedge formation at the end of 1992 was upwards. The wedge is pointing downwards. The wedge is well defined, since there are five troughs lying close to or on the base and four peaks lying on or close to the upper side. There was a false break-out in January 1995, when the price rose quickly from the upper side at 326p to a peak at 362p. The price made little progress, and eventually re-entered the wedge in July 1995. The price left the wedge permanently in November 1995 at 270p and meandered downwards to 210p at the time of writing. Thus the true break-out was such as to reverse the direction of the price when it entered the wedge.

If further proof is needed of the rule that a wedge formation is usually a reversal formation, then it is provided by Guinness, as shown in Figure 9.16. Here the downwards pointing wedge took almost a year in its formation. There are five peaks which lie on or close to the upper side

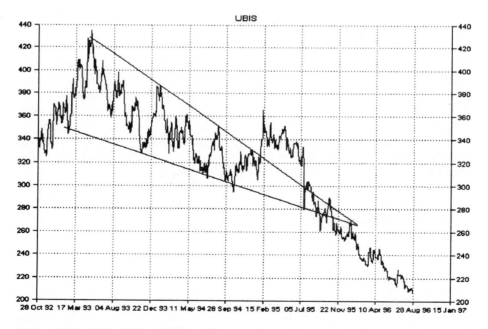

Figure 9.15 United Biscuits has a downward pointing wedge covering three years of price movement

Figure 9.16 Guinness has a downward pointing wedge covering just over a year of price movement. The price direction is the opposite from that when it entered the wedge

and three troughs along its base. Following the first trough in July 1994 at 430p, the price rose rapidly to the top of the wedge at 502p, although of course the wedge was not defined at the time. There are a further two peaks on the upper side of the wedge before the next trough was formed to enable the base of the wedge to be defined. Before the wedge was left behind, there were two more peaks and a trough lying on the sides.

The break-out from this wedge was certainly dramatic. The price left via the upper side in March 1995 at 420p, and within a few days had climbed to 470p, before rising eventually to over 530p.

FLAGS

Flags are very short term periods of hesitation which follow a rapid rise or rapid fall in the price. They are mini-equivalents of triangles and rectangles, but in the latter case they are more often parallelograms than rectangles. They should last for no more than three weeks before the price resumes its previous direction. Thus they differ from most of the hesitation patterns discussed in that the most likely future direction of the price is known. The extent of the future movement is usually equal to the distance which the price has already moved up or down the flagpole to the flag. Thus the flag can be considered to be an area halfway up the flagpole.

The Allied Domecq share price shows two flags following two sharp price rises (Figure 9.17). The first occurs in September 1993, following the rise from 545p. The price spent a few days bouncing between the 590p and 600p levels before continuing upwards to 632p. This is a case where the flag is not halfway up the flagpole, but rather nearer to the top. However, the second flag in this chart is closer to the ideal. The price rose rapidly from the base at 550p to form a flag in the 612p to 632p area. After a few days of indecision, the price rose rapidly again to 691p.

It should be noted that flags behave in the expected sense of the sharp rise or fall continuing further on about seven occasions out of 10. Even in the chart of Allied Domecq, a false flag can be seen in the price fall from 615p in April 1994. The price appeared to form a flag at the 565p level, but did not fall any further. Rather it moved sharply upwards to 590p, just about halving the extent of the previous fall.

A more well-behaved version of a flag can be seen in the chart of Grand Metropolitan in Figure 9.18. At the time of writing the price rose almost vertically from 428p to the 450p to 455p area where it spent just a few days. It then rose again almost vertically to another flag at 475p to 477p. Thus the first flag is almost exactly halfway up the flagpole. The movement from the second flag is yet to be resolved.

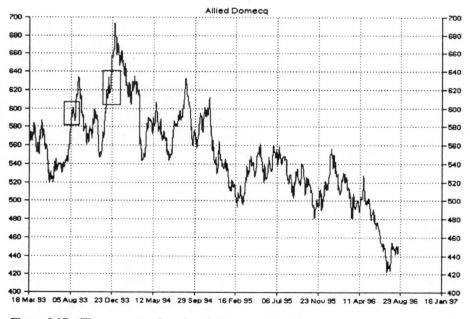

Figure 9.17   There are two flags in this chart of Allied Domecq

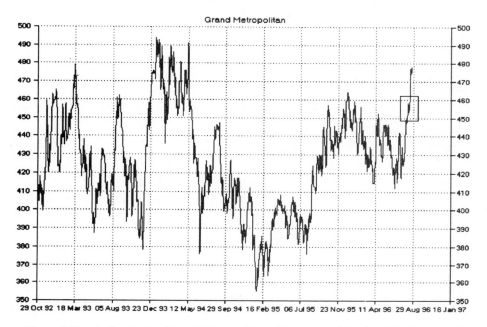

Figure 9.18   A flag in the Grand Metropolitan share price. The final flag is yet to be resolved

British Gas, shown in Figure 9.19, is an excellent example of a false flag. The price fell rapidly in May 1996 from 232p to the 172p to 180p area, where it stayed for a few days. The normal expectation from this point would be for a further fall of perhaps another 50p, but the price rebounded slightly from this level, thereby spoiling the flag formation.

EARTHQUAKES

There are quite a few examples of earthquake formations in the top 100 or so shares over the last five years. Such formations are characterised by a sharp fall over no more than a few days, and an equally sharp rise some months or even more than a year later. These contrast with the more common sharp bottom formations, in which the price spends only a few days in the trough before rising again. Where a share has suffered a sharp fall, the investor can therefore be on the look-out for a corresponding rise at a later date. An investor will be unable to capitalise on such a rise as it occurs, because it will occur over one or perhaps two or three days at the most, giving no time to react. The value to the investor is that the extent of the rise is usually equal to the extent of the fall, and while occasionally the rise is a little less than this, it never seems to be greater. The investor

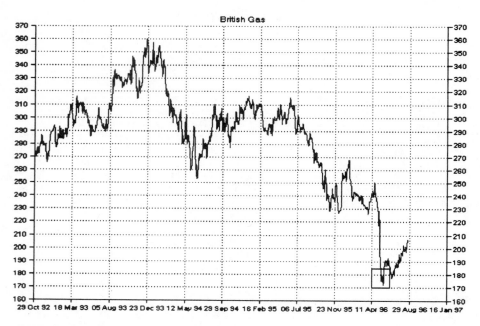

Figure 9.19 Sometimes the price rebounds from the position of a flag, as in British Gas

should not buy immediately after the initial fall, but should wait to see that the price has stabilised and is not going to fall any further. Since the corresponding rise will occur at some indeterminate point in the future, the investor may have to wait a relatively long time before the profit accumulates.

A good example of a short term earthquake can be seen for P&O in Figure 9.20. The price fell sharply over the course of a few days in September 1995, from 550p to 464p, i.e. a fall of 86p. A few months later in January 1996, the price rose equally sharply from 463p to 562p, i.e. rise of 99p.

Reverse Earthquakes

As might be expected, there is a counterpart to the earthquake formation in which the price rises sharply over the course of a few days, and then some time later, falls equally sharply. These are not to be confused with sharp, spike tops, in which the price spends only a few days at the new level before falling back. An example is shown in the chart of Glaxo-Wellcome in Figure 9.21. The price rose rapidly in November 1995 from just below 800p to 852p in a day. The price then continued upwards at a much slower pace to reach a peak at 967p before falling to 908p. It was

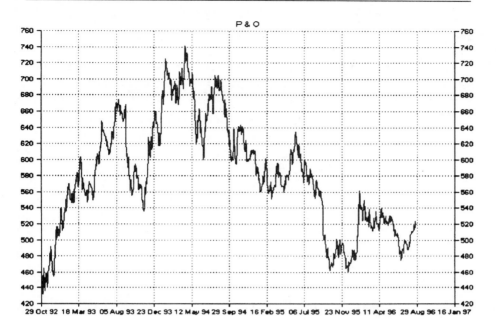

Figure 9.20   An earthquake formation in the chart of P&O

Figure 9.21   A reverse earthquake in the chart of Glaxo-Wellcome

from this point that the second leg of the reverse earthquake was formed, the price falling in two days to 812p. Thus the formation is not quite symmetrical, with the rise of 55p being much less than the fall of 96p.

An investor holding this share should not have been caught by this fall, since the price at the point the fall occurred (908p) was already more than 5% down from the peak value of 967p. The use of a stop loss would have prevented such a loss.

10

Moving Averages

Moving averages and the way in which they can be calculated were discussed briefly in Chapter 2. It was also pointed out that moving averages were smoothing devices which removed fluctuations of periodicity equal to or less than the span used for the average. The result of the smoothing process can then be considered to be a 'better' representation of the movement of the share price than the actual share price data. The greater the span of the average which is used, the smoother is the resulting plot.

A good example to illustrate the effect of various moving averages is the chart of the BPB Industries share price, a history from the beginning of 1983 being shown in Figure 10.1. It is a good example because of the large amount of cyclic movement which is obviously present.

A commonly used moving average is one of 200 days, and this is used to isolate the underlying longer term trends in a share price history. As was mentioned above, an average removes fluctuations of periodicity less than or equal to the span of the average. Thus we would expect a 200-day moving average to remove cycles of wavelength of 200 days or less. Looking again at the chart in Figure 10.1, we can see that the cycles which are in evidence for the period since early 1988 have trough-to-trough or peak-to-peak distances which are about half a year or less, i.e. their wavelengths are half a year, about 120 business days. Thus on the basis of what we have just said, we would expect these to be removed by a 200-day average. On the other hand, the large cyclical movement which had peaks in October 1987 (just prior to the crash) and again in early 1994 has a wavelength of nearly seven years. Thus we would not expect this cycle to be removed by a 200-day average.

That this approach is correct can be seen by the shape of the 200-day average of the BPB share price which is illustrated in Figure 10.2. As predicted, the cycles which were visible since 1988 have for the most part been removed, but the cycle which has its peaks in 1987 and 1994 can still be seen.

By the same argument, the use of a shorter span moving average such as 20 days would result in the removal of cycles of 20 days or less wavelength. Since most of the cycles which are present since 1988 have wavelengths of

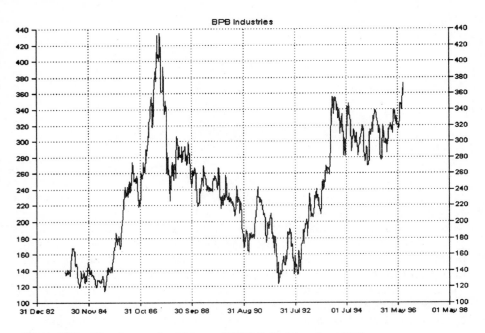

Figure 10.1   The share price history of BPB Industries since 1983

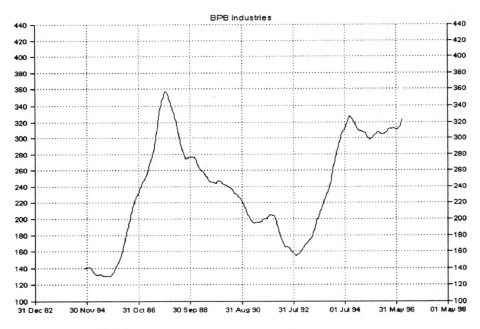

Figure 10.2   The 200-day moving average of the BPB share price since 1983

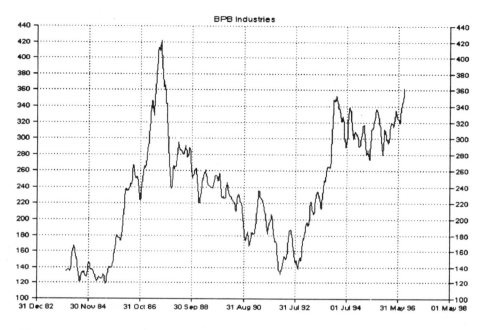

Figure 10.3 The 20-day moving average of the BPB share price since 1983

much more than 20 days, we would not expect these to be removed by such an average, although we would expect to lose the random day-do-day movement and any cycles which have very short wavelengths of less than 20 days. That this does indeed happen can be seen quite clearly from the plot of the 20-day moving average of the BPB share price in Figure 10.3.

In order to get a clear idea of the smoothing effect of a moving average, the final few months of the BPB share price are shown in Figure 10.4 with the 20-day average superimposed. In this case, in order to preserve the relationship between the data and the average, the average has been offset half a span back in time. In this mode of plotting, the average is directly superimposable upon the data (see the chapter on channel analysis). It can now be seen that the average is the best smooth line drawn through the data so that the very short term fluctuations are removed.

These few examples should serve to put into perspective the reasons for selecting particular spans. For the trader interested in short term movements, it is essential that cycles of short wavelength are not removed from the data. Thus a short span average, for example of 10–50 days, must be used in order to preserve such cycles while removing the day-to-day variations. On the other hand, the longer term investor is more interested in the long term underlying trends and not in the shorter term trends. Thus these short term trends can be removed and the longer term trends highlighted by selecting averages such as 200 or 240 days.

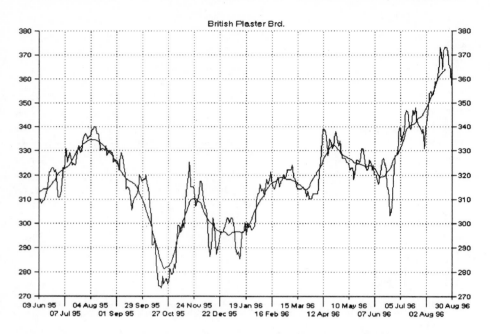

Figure 10.4   The 20-day moving average and the BPB share price since June 1995. The average is plotted half a span back in time so as to show that the average is a smoother version of the price itself

MOVING AVERAGE APPLICATIONS

There are almost as many ways of applying moving averages as there are investors who use them. The four main methods are:

- Buying and selling when the share price crosses the moving average
- Buying and selling when one moving average crosses another
- Buying and selling when a moving average changes direction
- Using an average to give the current state of an underlying trend, usually long term.

Price Crossing a Single Average

In this method, as in all other methods discussed in this chapter, moving averages are plotted with no lag, i.e. the latest calculated point is plotted on the time axis at the same place in time as the latest data point used to calculate it. Thus the average and the data will always end at the same point in time.

   The signal to buy is when the share price, which will have been running below the smoother average line, crosses up through this line, and conversely the time to sell will be when the price falls down through the average line. Some investors use this method only for generating a buying signal and do not use it for selling. They use methods such as a stop loss in order to secure the profit from the rising share price or to terminate a trade which fails to generate a profit in the first place.

A derivative of this price crossing method is to use two averages. The second, longer span average is not used in conjunction with crossing by the share price, but is used to modify the buying or selling decision generated by crossing of the first average. Thus a share will only be bought when a buying signal is generated if this second average is in a rising mode, and a share will not be sold if this longer term average is in a falling mode. Use of this second average therefore comes under the fourth category in the above list, where it is used solely to give an indication of the underlying trend. Used in this way, this will naturally reduce the number of buying and selling opportunities compared with the use of just a single average.

The only decision which has to be made with the single average method is the span to be used for the moving average. While, as we have stated, a 200-day moving average will leave only the long term trends visible, we will find that such an average is unsuitable for the method because of the time lag associated with it. Being much smoother than a short term average, it is much slower to respond to a rise or fall in the share price than a short term average. This fact can be demonstrated by two examples, one in which a crossing of the 200-day average is used as a buying or selling signal, and one in which a crossing of a 50-day average is used for the signals.

Figure 10.5 shows the share price of BPB since the beginning of 1994, and superimposed upon this is a 200-day moving average. The vertical lines below the average indicate points where the price broke up through the average, i.e. generated buying signals. The vertical lines above the average indicate points where the price fell down through the average, i.e. generated selling signals. Thus we can see that during the period in question there were seven buying signals and six selling signals. Of the six pairs of buying/selling transactions, half of these gave a selling signal at a price lower than the previous buying signal, i.e. the investor would have lost money in all but one transaction. Thus quite obviously a 200-day average is far too unresponsive for such a method to succeed.

Figure 10.6 shows a similar chart but with the average now reduced in span to 50 days. This time there were 11 complete transactions, now split as five losers and six winners. Thus it has given a slight advantage to move the span of the average to shorter periods. Notice also that the buying signals in Figure 10.6 that have a direct equivalent in Figure 10.5 occur considerably earlier in time.

It might appear that it would be an advantage to move to even shorter averages, such as 20-day or 10-day. The problem in doing this is that the number of false signals, i.e. those occasions where the price crosses the

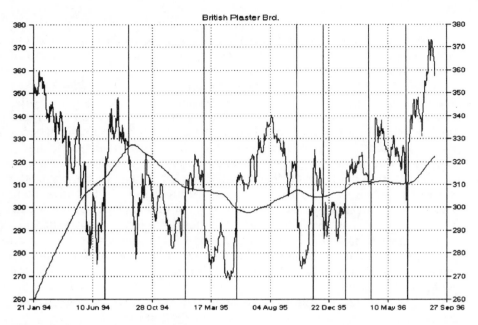

Figure 10.5 Crossings of the 200-day moving average and the BPB share price since 1994

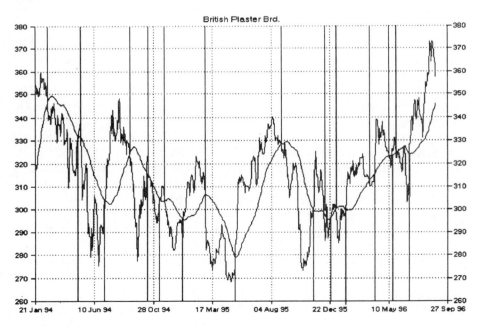

Figure 10.6 Crossings of the 50-day moving average and the BPB share price since 1994

average only to recross it in the opposite direction a few days later, increases dramatically. Such situations obviously lead to losses. This leads to the conclusion that a little research has to be done to determine the optimum average for a particular share. With a computer system this is an easy task, but if averages are calculated manually, then it is daunting to compute, say, 10 different averages for one share. It will usually be found to be the case that an average somewhere between 30 and 50 days will give the best results, i.e. the greatest overall gain. In order to get an appreciation of the price movement that occurs between buying and selling signals, the dates of the buying and selling signals and the share prices at those dates for the 50-day average in the case of BPB are shown in Table 10.1. These of course correspond to the signals shown in Figure 10.6. Note that there are three occasions where there was a false signal in the sense that the selling signal occurred less than 10 days after the buying signal. In such cases the chances that the price makes a significant advance are small. Two of these three cases saw a small loss and one just a penny rise.

Note that the five losing situations gave only small losses, while the winning situations gave slightly larger gains. If dealing costs are ignored the percentage gain over the 11 transactions is 2.1%. If dealing costs are applied to the figures, then the investor would have come out with a very small loss.

The last column of Table 10.1 shows the status of the 200-day average. As mentioned above, the status of such a long term average is often used as a modifier to the buying or selling signal. As a buying modifier, it is used to confirm a buy if it is rising, but negate a buy if it is falling. The opposite view is taken for selling decisions, although it is unusual to use this method for other than buying decisions. As can be seen from Table 10.1, used in this way only six buying decisions would have been made, and five of these would have made gains.

Table 10.1 Dates and prices for buying and selling signals generated by the BPB share price crossing the 50-day average

Date	Buying price	Date	Selling price	200-day average
03/05/94	334	09/05/94	329	Rising
05/07/94	304	31/08/94	324	Rising
12/10/94	320	14/10/94	314	Falling
10/11/94	304	23/11/94	303	Falling
06/01/95	299	28/02/95	294	Falling
11/05/95	284	29/08/95	325	Rising
14/11/95	298	08/12/95	297	Falling
27/12/95	298	05/01/96	299	Rising
30/01/96	299	26/03/96	311	Rising
08/04/96	312	13/05/96	322	Rising
17/05/96	321	29/05/96	323	Falling

The BPB case was chosen particularly to illustrate situations where the use of the average crossing method is not very successful and to show why this is the case. This approach is a necessary one, since an investor should always be aware of the reasons for a method failing in order to be able to correct for it. The BPB situation, with its very cyclical behaviour over the past two years, has offered, at least theoretically, good profit-making prospects for investors who could time the buying and selling decisions correctly. The cycles have given price rises of between 20% and 30%.

The reason for the poor performance of the method in the BPB case is simple. It is because the price rose rapidly from the troughs and fell back rapidly from the peaks. With a rapid rise, the price overshoots the rising average by a large amount, thereby limiting the proportion of the rise which is captured by the investor. At the other end of the transaction, a rapid fall has the same effect, the price having fallen a considerable distance from the peak before the selling decision is triggered. As was mentioned above, although the obvious fix for this problem would seem to lie with a reduction in the span of the average, so that the average begins to rise or fall much sooner, this is negated by an increase in the number of false signals.

Where the average crossing method does score is in those situations where the share price has tended to follow gentler but more sustained rises. In these cases the price crosses the average at a much more reasonable rate so that the investor is not faced with a large gap between the average and the price at the time of the buying signal. A good example of such a successful application of the crossing method is shown by the share price of British Petroleum where a 200-day average is superimposed (Figure 10.7). Here we have a sustained rise in price from late 1992. Since the price crossed up through the average before the first date on the chart, the investor would already be holding the share in late 1992. As can be seen, the price virtually doubled before the selling signal was given. Even this can be considered to be a false signal, since the dip below the average was of a temporary nature, the price then continuing to climb.

The general conclusion from this discussion of the average crossing method is that although it is widely used, a great deal of research is required to find the best average for a particular share, and even then, the results over a long period are not particularly startling.

Two Averages Crossing

As was pointed out above, one difficulty with the price/average crossing method is that fairly short term fluctuations in the share price can take it above and below the average repeatedly, giving false signals which lose the investor money. One way around this is to use the crossing of two averages. The shorter term average is used as a substitute for the price, and since it will now be smoother than the price fluctuations, there should be

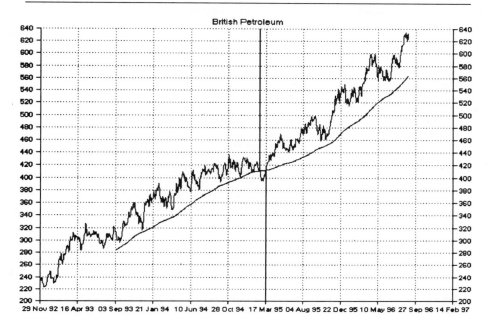

Figure 10.7 The price crossings of the 200-day average for the British Petroleum share price. The sustained rise in the share price kept the number of crossings down

fewer false signals given. The penalty for this improvement will be that the shorter term average will have lost some speed of response when compared with the price itself, and therefore there will be a longer lag time until the signal is given. This will reduce the effective gain which can be made from the transaction. As with all stock market investment, what we have is a method of reducing the risk which will always result in a reduced return.

As a start, we can take two averages which are fairly widely spaced. Thus a 200-day average will give a good indication of the longer term trend, and a 50-day average should give a reasonably smooth crossing average. Figure 10.8 shows that the number of buying and selling signals is now reduced to four, but that there is only one matched pair of a buying signal followed by a selling signal. If the first buying signal on 28th July 1995 is examined more closely, it will be seen that it lags well behind the points at which the price crosses the 50-day average and then the 200-day average. This delay is so serious that the price has risen to 310.5p on 30th June 1995 from the low point of 269p before the signal is given. The corresponding selling point is not given until 10th November 1995, when the price is down to 297p from a high of 340p. Thus although the share price showed an excellent rise between April and August 1995 of 26% (269p to 340p), this method resulted in a loss of 4.3%. So we can conclude

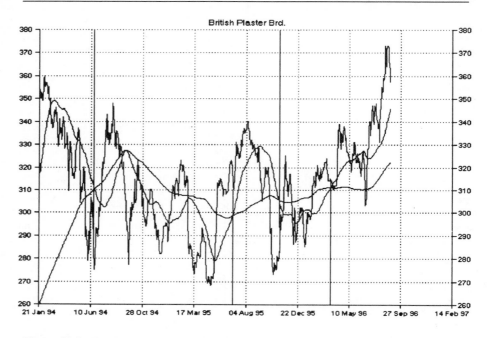

Figure 10.8 Buying and selling signals generated by crossing of the 50-day and 200-day moving averages of the BPB share price

that the averages employed were of far too long a span to give any sensitivity to the price rise and fall.

Moving to shorter term averages, Figure 10.9 shows the effect of using a 10-day average and a 50-day average. Taking the June to November cycle first, it can be seen that the buying point occurs much further back in time, occurring on 26th May 1995 when the price was 314p. This compares with 310.5p on 30th June in the previous example. In this case, although the decision point occurred sooner, unfortunately, due to the rapid short term movements in the price, a slightly inferior buying price was indicated.

The selling point was also moved back to a point nearer to the peak price, occurring on 8th September at 323p, compared with 10th November at 297p in the previous example. We have now captured a gain of about 3% compared with a loss of 4.3%. Following this particular buying/selling operation, there are three more pairs, each giving a small loss.

There is a way in which the two averages crossing method can be improved dramatically, and that is by buying only at a crossing point if both averages are rising. Such crossing points have been called 'golden crosses'. Their effect in the BPB case is to rule out these last three losing transactions, leaving only the first one with the small gain.

This example of BPB has been chosen because it is a difficult one, stretching these moving averages methods to the limit. It is useful to

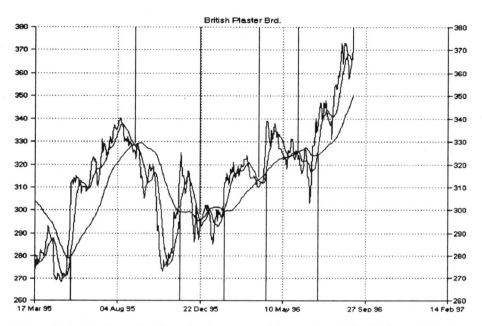

Figure 10.9 Buying and selling signals generated by crossing of the 10-day and 50-day moving averages of the BPB share price

compare this with a well-behaved example in which golden crosses give useful profits. Such an example is shown in Figure 10.10, with the 10- and 50-day averages shown for British Steel. The short term average is rather difficult to see because it remains fairly close to the share price itself.

There are eight golden crosses shown where the two averages cross, with the proviso that both averages are rising at the time the crossing occurs. In six of the crosses, the price rise which follows is quite profitable. In the second and third crosses from the beginning of the chart, the price rise in the days before the cross is so rapid that the price is at its peak at the time of the cross. In such cases, the price begins to fall at the very time the buy signal is being given. Even so, to be given six good buying signals out of eight has to be considered a vindication of the method in the case of British Steel.

It must be emphasised, however, that each share behaves differently, and a true evaluation of any of the methods discussed here can only be made with a great deal of effort across a large number of shares.

Change in Direction of an Average

The principle behind this method is that moving averages isolate trends. The type of trend being isolated, i.e. whether it is short, medium or long

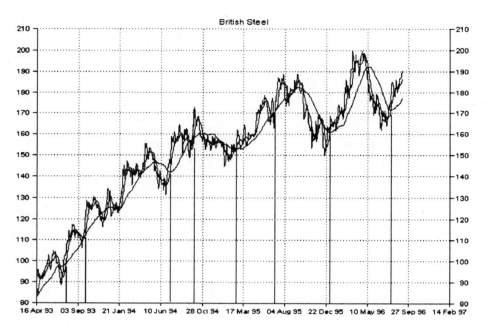

Figure 10.10   The British Steel share price: golden crosses where 10-day and 50-day averages cross and both are rising

term, depends entirely upon the span of the average being used. Once an average changes direction, then the trends of longer periodicity than the span of the average have also changed direction. How long they remain running in the new direction cannot be determined, since a subsequent reversal of direction will depend upon random factors. It is sufficient to know that the end of a trend will be signalled in exactly the same way as its beginning, viz. by a change in the direction of the appropriate moving average.

As with any other moving average method, the crucial factor is the span used for the average which is being used as an indicator. Large spans will isolate long term trends, but the delay in a change of direction of the average will mean that a considerable portion of the ensuing price rise or price fall will have already occurred. In the author's book *Stocks and Shares Simplified* the use of two averages was advocated, a 5-week (25-day) average for those investors who wished to take advantage of very short term trends, and a 13-week (65-day) average for those investors who had longer term ambitions. It was also pointed out that while the shorter average captured more of the gain, it also gave more false signals.

As an example, a plot of BPB with the 25-day average is shown in Figure 10.11. The turning points in the average are marked by vertical lines, those in the top half being the selling signals, and those in the bottom

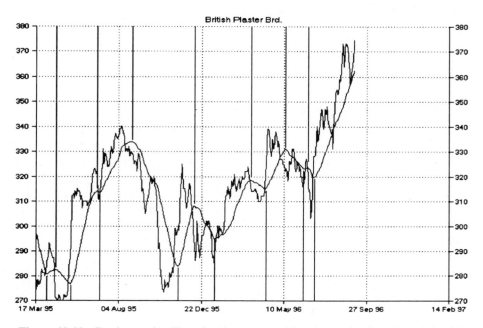

Figure 10.11 Buying and selling signals generated by change in direction of the 25-day moving average of BPB

Table 10.2 Buying and selling points in the BPB share price in Figure 10.11

Date	Buying price	Date	Selling price
04/04/95	286	19/04/95	271
15/05/95	288	30/06/95	310.5
04/07/95	317	25/08/95	329
13/11/95	300	11/12/95	291
16/01/96	296	14/03/96	315
09/04/96	322	15/05/96	323
14/06/96	321	20/06/96	324
02/07/96	328		

half the buying signals. There are seven possible complete transactions, and these are listed in Table 10.2. The overall percentage gain for these transactions was just under 1.6%.

This author has always held the view that taken across a large number of shares, the average turning point method is superior to the other moving average methods discussed here because of its more fundamental nature. It is focusing attention on the behaviour of trends and especially on their turning points. It will be most successful for those shares in which trends persist for the longest, and these shares can be discovered by simple in-spection of their moving averages to pin-point those which have the fewest turning points over their price history for a given average such as 25 days or 65 days.

WHY MOVING AVERAGE METHODS ARE ONLY PARTIALLY SUCCESSFUL

We have already mentioned that the mathematically correct way of pres-enting moving averages is with the average plotted half a span back in time, and Figure 10.4 was used to illustrate that when presented in this way, it can be seen quite clearly that the centred average is a smooth representation of the data itself. *The centred average thus represents the underlying trend of the share price when the shorter term movements which otherwise confuse the picture are removed.*

When plotted in this way, we can see that there is a gap of half of the span of the average between the last plotted point of the average and the last share price, as shown in Figure 10.12. In the figure a 51-week average

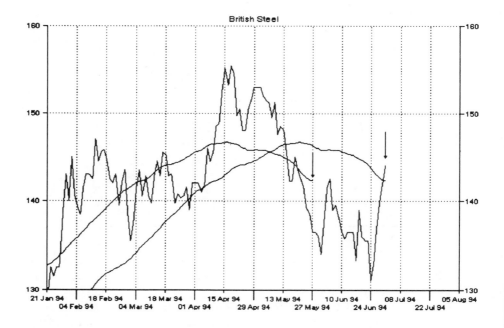

Figure 10.12 Both unlagged and centred 51-day moving averages plotted for British Steel. The centred average terminates on 27th May 1994, and the unlagged average on 1st July 1994

is plotted, in both centred and unlagged forms. The last data point is at 1st July 1994, and the last plotted point of the centred average is at 27th May 1994. Thus we have no knowledge of the behaviour of the trend in prices in this gap. Any deduction that we make about the underlying trend at the time of the last data point is therefore only an estimate.

Now we can see quite clearly why moving average methods are only correct some of the time. We are interested in the trends in share prices, and use moving averages as a substitute for the trend itself. Moreover, we are anxious to know the state of the trend at this exact moment in time. However, what is hidden in the way moving averages are normally presented when plotted with no lag is the fact that the latest value of the average is telling us what the trend was doing half a span ago in time, and not what it is doing now. Thus in Figure 10.12, the obvious deduction from the unlagged average which is plotted up to date is that the trend is continuing to fall, but this deduction may or may not be correct.

In the present example, the future course of the trend is given by the centred average in Figure 10.13. We can now see that the trend, as represented by the 51-day moving average, changed direction on 6th June 1994. Thus, the trend was rising on 1st July 1994, showing that the deduction of a falling trend from the direction of the unlagged average in Figure 10.12 was incorrect.

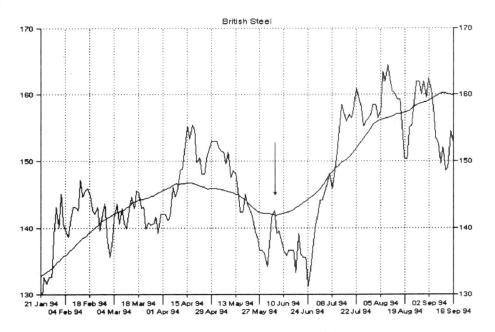

Figure 10.13 Data are now plotted further into the future. We can see that the centred average, representing the trend, reversed direction on 6th June 1994

Taking the chart in Figure 10.14, we can see that the centred average terminated on 10th March 1995, while the unlagged average terminated at the last data point on 14th April 1995. The deduction, which may or may not be correct, is that since the unlagged average is rising on 14th April, so is the trend. Moving further into the future, we can see from the chart in Figure 10.15 that in this case, the deduction from the direction of the unlagged average on 14th April that the trend is still rising turned out to be correct.

Thus we have seen one example where the trend reversed direction, and was going the opposite way to the direction indicated by the unlagged moving average, and one example in which the trend was going the same way as the unlagged moving average. The moving average methods as described in this chapter all make the incorrect assumption that the moving average tells us what the trend is doing now; in other words that if the average is rising, then the current trend is rising. We can now see why this assumption can be incorrect.

The advantage of using the average turning point as an indicator of a change in the direction of the trend is that, since the turning point is as close as half a span in the past, the trend is less likely to have reversed direction by the current time. We can estimate the probability of being

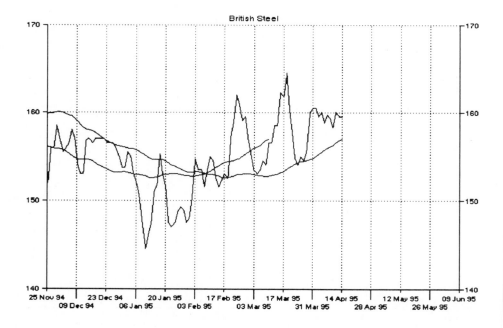
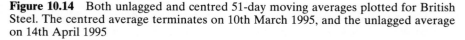

Figure 10.14 Both unlagged and centred 51-day moving averages plotted for British Steel. The centred average terminates on 10th March 1995, and the unlagged average on 14th April 1995

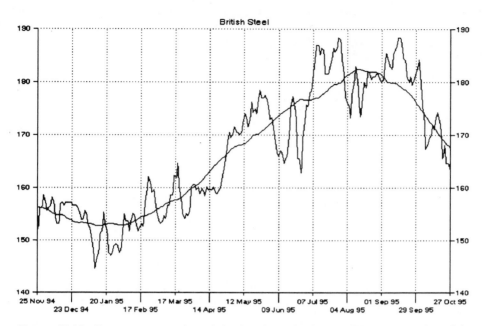

Figure 10.15 Data are now plotted further into the future. We can see that the centred average, representing the trend, maintained the same direction

correct or incorrect easily from historical data by measuring the length of time for which trends maintain the same direction. This can be done by marking the turning points in a plot of a moving average and measuring the distances between successive turns.

Where the majority of these lengths of time are less than half of the number of points used in the moving average, then we are more likely to be incorrect than correct in using the new direction of the moving average as an indication of the current direction of the trend. Thus, using a 51-day average, we run into trouble if many of the turning points are closer together in time than 26 days. This gives us a useful yardstick by which shares can be compared with each other. Some will have a history of more persistent trends, making them good candidates for moving average methods, while others will have many more short-lived trends, making them dangerous to the investor.

From this approach, we can now explain why BPB gave vastly inferior results to those obtained by British Steel, using a 50-day average. An analysis of both histories from the beginning of 1992 to date showed 17 turning points in the 50-day average of BPB. The average time between turning points, i.e. persistence of trends, was 46 days, and seven of these intervals were less than 26 days. On the other hand, British Steel gave only 11 turning points in the same period of time, with an average persistence of 73 days. Only two of these were of less than 26 days. Thus British Steel trends lasted more than half as long again as BPB trends, with an obvious implication for profitability when averages are used to signal buying points.

11

Relative Strength and Momentum

In *Stocks and Shares Simplified* it was pointed out that a knowledge of general market conditions was essential to the making of buying and selling decisions for specific shares. When the general trend of the market is downwards the reasons for buying a particular share must be overpowering, since sooner or later most shares get caught up in the ebb tide. The performance of a share relative to the market in general is thus an important yardstick. Fortunately we have available to us a simple but powerful means of measuring this relative performance in the Relative Strength Index.

Another useful piece of information about a share is the head of steam that has been built up behind a rise; this is best interpreted by the concept of momentum. There are several indicators which measure momentum, and the Welles Wilder Index is probably the most popular.

RELATIVE STRENGTH INDEX (RSI)

The Relative Strength Index is simple if laborious to calculate. It is simply the ratio of the share price to a broadly based index such as the All Share Index or the FTSE100 Index calculated from day to day. The RSI is then plotted on the same chart as the share price. The actual values for the RSI are unimportant, so that the scale for these can be omitted from the plot. This is not done in the examples here because the RSI has been plotted in a separate box in order to enlarge the trends for easier reading.

As an example to get an idea of the appearance of an RSI, this index is plotted, along with the share price for Boots, from the beginning of 1983 in Figure 11.1. It can be seen that although there are similarities between the RSI in the upper panel and the share price in the lower panel in that some peaks coincide, for the most part the two have a different appearance. Note that the scale used for the vertical axis of the RSI has no significance; it is the shape that we are interested in.

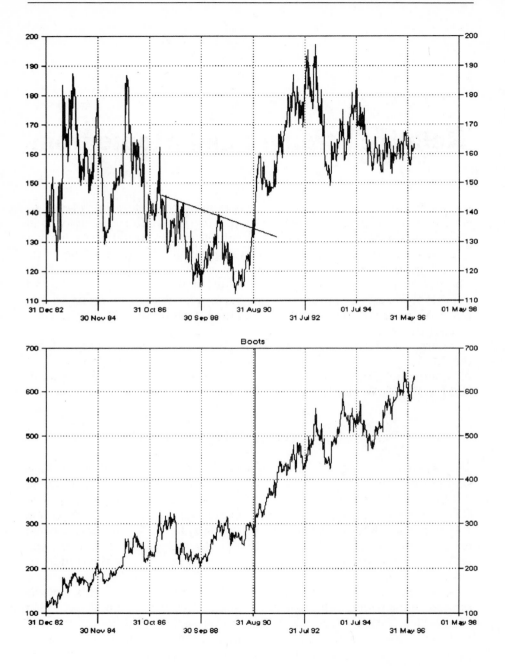

Figure 11.1 The Boots share price (lower panel) with the Relative Strength Index (upper panel). The latter uses the FTSE100 Index as the base

When the RSI is increasing, this means that the share price is outper-forming the market, while when it is decreasing, the share price is under-performing the market. Thus in Figure 11.1, prior to mid-1990 the general trend of the RSI is downwards, showing that Boots was underperforming the market. From the low point in mid-1990, the RSI rose rapidly, when Boots greatly outperformed the market. Over the final year, the RSI oscillated within a narrow band, broadly following the market.

While these rises and falls in the share performance are interesting, they are not very helpful in themselves. It is the application of charting tech-niques, especially the use of trendlines, that makes the RSI a powerful tool for the determination or confirmation of buying and selling points. Such a trendline has been drawn on the RSI in Figure 11.1 to highlight a down-trend that started in early 1987 and continued until October 1990. There are four sharp peaks lying on this line. As with charts of share prices themselves, we can signal the end of such a downtrend by observing the penetration of the trendline as was the case with share prices. It is useful, as with share prices, to avoid false signals by using a 3% penetration as a criterion. This penetration by 3% above the downtrend was achieved on 5th October 1990. This date is shown by the vertical line drawn on the lower share price chart, and corresponds to a share price of 312p.

That this is a very useful buying point for Boots shares can be seen by the fact that the price rose consistently with only minor falls to about 480p over the course of the next 18 months.

It should be noted that it would be difficult to establish this buying point simply from the chart of the share price itself. Although it appears that a resistance line could be drawn at about the 310p level, the peaks that would compose such a line would vary by rather more than 3% around the line, making it a rather questionable resistance.

An example of a rising trend line in an RSI is shown in Figure 11.2 for Anglian Water. The uptrend from March to December 1995 is a very strong trend, since there are six troughs which fall on or very close to it. It can be seen that the trendline is decisively penetrated in January 1996. The RSI had fallen more than 3% below the trendline on 17th January 1996, at which point the share price was 572p. This would therefore give a selling signal for those investors not using the stop loss method. Over the next few days the price fell slightly to 566p, giving the investor confidence that the signal was correct. This confidence seemed to be slightly misplaced when the price rose again within a few days to 590p and even more misplaced when following a further fall the price rose even higher to 612p over the next few weeks. However, a look at the chart for the first half of 1996 shows that the investor would have been happy to be out of the share, since the switchback rise saw rapid swings of nearly 100p in the price.

It is interesting that the straight uptrend in the RSI has been derived from a curved uptrend over the same period of time in the share price. As we saw in Chapter 8, penetration of curved trends is slightly more

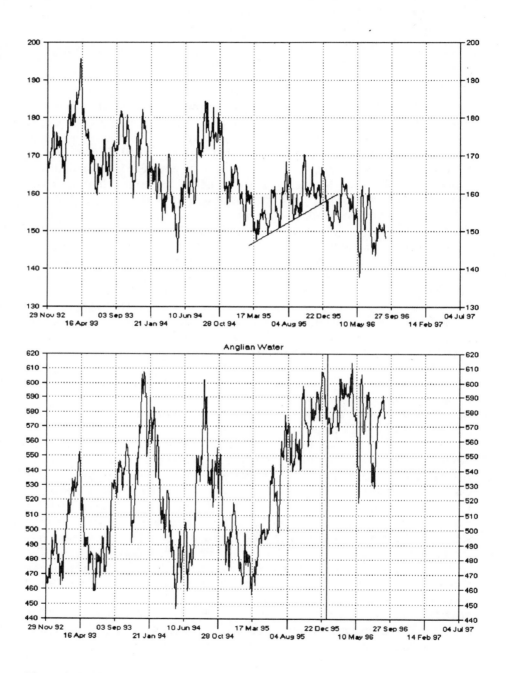

Figure 11.2 The Anglian Water share price (lower panel) with the Relative Strength Index (upper panel). The latter uses the FTSE100 Index as the base

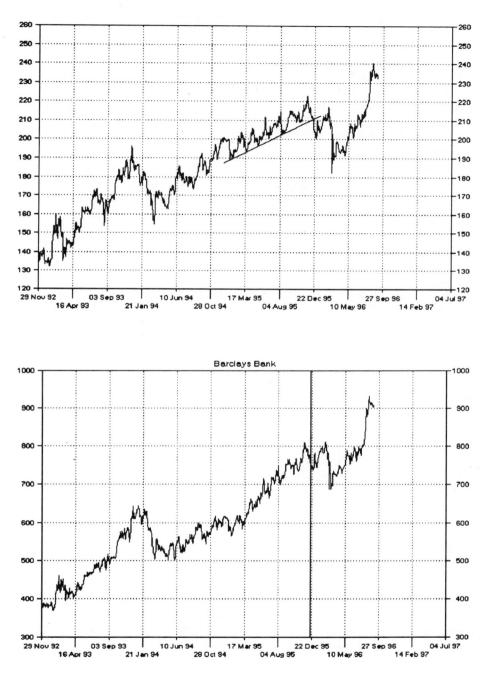

Figure 11.3 The Barclays share price (lower panel) with the Relative Strength Index (upper panel). The latter uses the FTSE100 Index as the base

subjective, since the curve has to be extrapolated, whereas penetration of a straight trendline is a much more positive event.

Barclays Bank (Figure 11.3) is another example of a curved uptrend in the share price being converted into a straight trendline by the RSI. The uptrend in the RSI has some six troughs lying on it, and was decisively penetrated at the end of December 1995. The share price at the time was 743p, and although it then recovered back to just over 800p, a larger fall occurred to 695p by March 1996. An investor who got out at 743p could therefore have bought back in at a much lower price, then enjoying a rise to above 900p in a very short space of time.

These few examples should serve to show the potential for the RSI method. Just as with the other indicators discussed in this book, there will be failures as well as successes, but the RSI has stood the test of time and is a useful addition to the range of indicators available to the investor.

THE WELLES WILDER INDEX (WWI)

This is one of several indicators which measure the momentum of a share price movement. As was shown in Chapter 2 where its calculation was outlined, it results in a value which always lies between zero and 100. The general consensus is that when the value falls below 30, the share in question is oversold, and can be bought, while if the value rises above 70 the share is overbought and should therefore be sold. Although any period can be used as the basis of the calculation, the accepted one is a 14-day period, and all the examples that follow use this value. A few examples here will serve to show circumstances in which the indicator has turned out to be useful.

The chart of the BAT share price with the 14-day WWI is shown in Figure 11.4. It can be seen that there is reasonable correlation between peaks and troughs in the share price and the points at which the WWI crosses the 70 and 30 levels.

There are several methods of using the WWI to generate buying and selling signals. Some investors use the method of buying or selling on an immediate cross of these levels. Others wait until the WWI has troughed if falling below 30 or peaked if rising above 70. Yet others wait for a recrossing of the level in the opposite direction before taking action.

The result of applying this first method, i.e. buying or selling on an initial crossing of the 30 and 70 lines, to BAT shares is shown in Figure 11.5. The points at which the WWI crosses the 30 or 70 levels are marked by vertical lines so that the corresponding point on the share price chart can be seen. Now that the chart scale has been enlarged, a very important property of the WWI can now be seen: the buying and selling signals usually occur before the turning point in the share price. This is quite marked for the trough in the BAT price that occurred at the end of May 1994. The buying

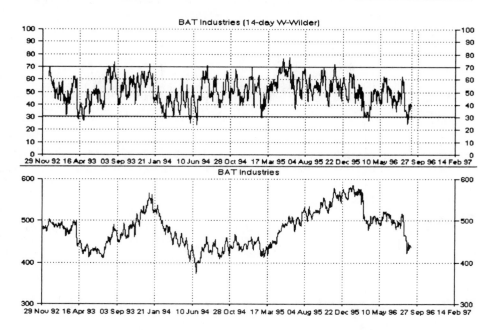

Figure 11.4 The BAT share price (lower panel) with the 14-day Welles Wilder Index (upper panel)

signal given by a crossing of the 30 line by the WWI occurred on 27th May, when the price was 410p. The actual trough in the share price occurred on 1st June 1994 when the price was 402p. The dates and corresponding share prices for the two complete buying and selling operations shown by the vertical lines in Figure 11.5 are listed in Table 11.1.

The average gain from the two transactions is 15.1%. This can be compared with the gain made by using the alternative method of buying and selling when the price crosses back up through the 30 level and back down through the 70 level. These points are shown in the chart in Figure 11.6. The dates and prices for these buying and selling operations are shown in Table 11.2. Now the average gain from the two transactions is 10.2%, an improvement over the first method. This is not always the case, and in practice there is not much difference between the two methods across a range of shares and a long timescale.

As with all other indicators discussed in this book, there are many occasions on which the Welles Wilder Index gives a false signal. British Steel (Figure 11.7) is a case in point. There are five points shown in the figure in which the WWI falls below 30% to indicate a buying opportunity. The first was on 10th October 1995, with the share price at 167.25p, and the next was on 3rd November 1995, with the price at 153p. Thus the price fell between the first and second signals. The lowest point reached by the

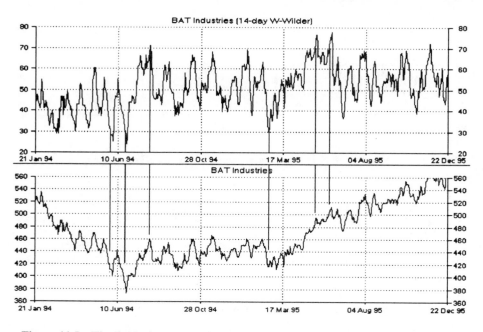

Figure 11.5 The BAT share price (lower panel) with the 14-day Welles Wilder Index (upper panel). Crossing points of the 30 and 70 levels are indicated by vertical lines

Table 11.1 Dates and prices for the buying and selling operations in BAT Industries as signalled by the WW Index crossing the 30 and 70 levels

Date	Buy at	Date	Sell at	% Gain
27/05/94	410	02/08/94	460	12.1
22/02/95	414	11/05/95	489	18.1

price was 150p on 18th December 1995, so that these two signals were very premature and would get the investor in above the bottom price. Since an investor would be acting on the first of these, there would have been a 10% loss by 18th December.

The selling signal came with a crossing of the 70% line on 26th February 1996, with the price at 182.5p. Again, this was premature, since the price reached 200p within a few weeks, but it did provide a useful profit for investors who bought around the 155p level the previous autumn.

The next three buying signals occurred on 11th May (at 184.5p), 21st May (176p) and 31st May (170p). Investors acting on the first of these would have been unhappy to see the price fall to its low of 162p on 27th June, i.e. a loss of 12.2%, before making a recovery to 190p.

It is not only with buying signals that the indicator can go wrong. The case of Zeneca is a spectacular example of multiple erroneous selling

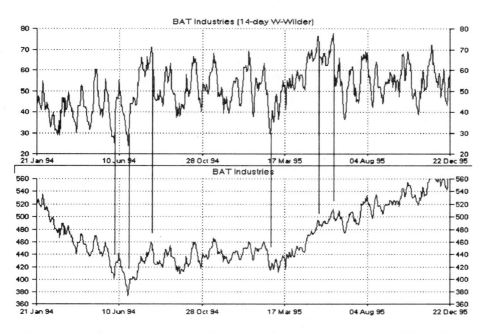

Figure 11.6 The BAT share price (lower panel) with the 14-day Welles Wilder Index (upper panel). Recrossing points of the 30 and 70 levels are indicated by vertical lines

Table 11.2 Dates and prices for the buying and selling operations in BAT Industries as signalled by the WW Index recrossing the 30 and 70 levels

Date	Buy at	Date	Sell at	% Gain
02/06/94	419	04/08/94	446	6.4
23/02/95	426	16/05/95	486	14.1

signals. In the chart shown in Figure 11.8, it can be seen that the share enjoyed a consistent rise from September 1993 to September 1996. An investor would not be pleased to be given selling signals when invested in this share. Nevertheless, the WWI gave no fewer than 10 such signals, starting with the first in July 1994 with the price at 738p. Successive signals were given when the price was 795p, 887p, 931p, 964p, 1081p, 1239p, 1402p and 1464p. The latest was on 19th August 1996 with the price at 1490p. Thus, not only were these signals false, but each occurred at a higher price than the previous one. The only one out of all of these signals which appears to have any justification in terms of a significant short term fall in share price is the one in November 1995 with the price at 1239p. The price rose from this point to 1322p before dipping again to 1224p. Even so, the investor selling at that point would still have seen a 100p rise over the next month before the minor fall.

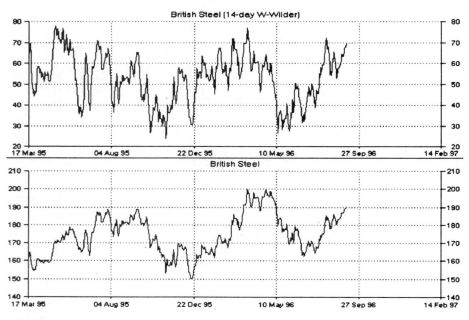

Figure 11.7 The British Steel share price (lower panel) with the 14-day Welles Wilder Index (upper panel)

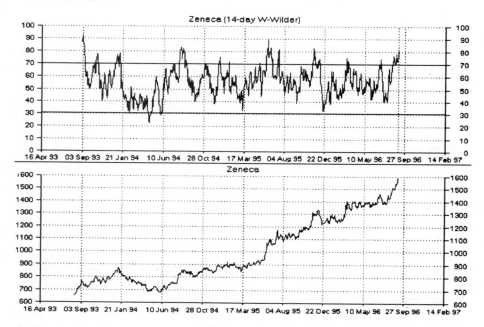

Figure 11.8 The Zeneca share price (lower panel) with the 14-day Welles Wilder Index (upper panel)

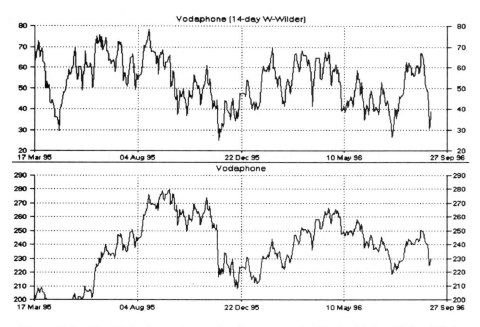

Figure 11.9 The Vodaphone share price (lower panel) with the 14-day Welles Wilder Index (upper panel). There is no sell signal given for the top in April 1996

It sometimes happens that the WWI does not give a signal even though there has been a reversal of the price. An example is shown for Vodaphone in Figure 11.9. From the low point in December 1995, the price rose via several short term cycles to reach a peak of 266.5p. However, the WWI did not breach the 70% line at around this time. An investor relying on the WWI to get him out of the share would see much of the profit slip away again, since the price fell back to 219p within a few months.

It is of interest to see how the WWI can deal with rapidly moving situations such as the earthquake formation given as an example previously in Chapter 9. This is shown for P&O in Figure 11.10. It would be expected that there would be a difficulty in dealing with such a fast moving change in share price. In this particular example, the earthquake commenced on 12th September 1995, with the price at 546p, and eventually the lowest price of 462p was reached on 11th October.

The WWI actually gave a buy signal on 13th September, showing that at that point the share was oversold. The price then was already on its way down to its low point. The investor buying simply on a fall of the WWI below 30% would thus come to grief. The damage would be somewhat less for those investors who buy on a recrossing of the 30% line, since by the time the WWI recrossed, the price was already much further down the landslide.

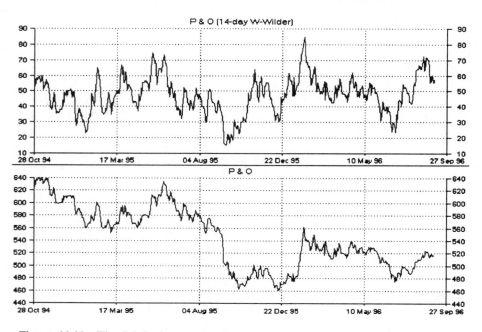

Figure 11.10 The P&O share price (lower panel) with the 14-day Welles Wilder Index (upper panel). As expected, the Welles Wilder Index cannot deal with an earthquake formation in the share price

The examples presented here serve to show the usefulness of the Welles Wilder Index in giving advance warning of the possibility of a trough or peak in the share price. They have shown that it can be dangerous to act solely when the WWI crosses the buying or selling levels of 30% and 70%. Much more success can be obtained with the WWI if, instead of buying or selling once the indicator crosses the 30% or 70% levels, the investor waits for the succeeding trough or peak before taking action.

12

The Rise–Fall Indicator

I first wrote about this indicator in *Stocks and Shares Simplified*, where it was shown to be excellent for getting investors in and out of shares close to the major troughs and peaks. It has been left out of later books for one reason only, and that is because of the great difficulty in programming it into a computer so as to generate the type of automatic buy and sell signals which are so readily produced by moving averages and other numerical indicators such as the Welles Wilder Index. The Rise–Fall Indicator (RFI) depends upon the breaking of trendlines, and therefore is entirely appropriate to a book such as this which is devoted to charting techniques.

The way in which the RFI is produced was discussed in Chapter 2. The previous value of the indicator is increased by one if the share price rises, is decreased by one if the share price falls, and stays unchanged if the share price is unchanged. The initial starting value for the indicator is set at some round number such as 100. From such a start it is extremely unlikely that the indicator will fall to anything approaching zero since to do this the share price would have to suffer 100 more falls than rises in the period in question. Even if it did fall to zero this would not affect the interpretation of the indicator.

Because the RFI is only concerned with whether a share price has fallen, risen or stayed still, and not with the actual price movement itself, it can be considered to be a trend indicator. While the trend sequence is maintained, for example rise, rise, fall, rise, rise, fall, the pattern of the indicator will continue to be repeated. When the pattern changes, as shown by the breaking of a trendline, then the trend has been broken, which usually implies a change in direction of the share price.

The overall impression of the RFI can be obtained from Figure 12.1 where the FTSE100 Index values and the indicator are shown. It can be seen that, in general, major troughs and peaks in the share price are accompanied by troughs and peaks in the indicator, but minor troughs and peaks may not be. The scale of the chart is such that the detail of the RFI cannot be seen.

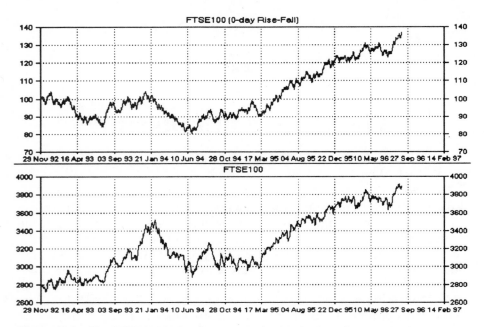

Figure 12.1   The FTSE100 Index (lower panel) with the RFI (upper panel)

Much more detail can be seen in the enlarged section of this chart, as shown in Figure 12.2. The RFI can now be seen to consist of many more peaks and troughs than the share price itself. Because of this larger number of peaks and troughs, the simple approach to drawing a trendline, i.e. that two troughs or two peaks are sufficient to define it, would lead to a large number of trendlines and a correspondingly large number of false buying and selling signals. With the RFI, it is essential that a minimum of three peaks or three troughs must lie on the trendline before it becomes valid. This reduces the number of buying and selling signals enormously.

Figure 12.2 is useful in showing how the indicator can be used to signal the beginning of a new trend. A downtrend line can be drawn in July 1993. This line is broken by the indicator on the 23rd, with the Index at this point being 2827.7. Note how successful the indicator was in signalling a change in direction with the Index only marginally above the lowest point reached a few days earlier. The FTSE100 Index climbed considerably higher from this point, reaching 3520.3 by 2nd February 1994 before falling back again.

The next big rise in the Index occurred from March 1995, and it is of interest to see how well the RFI performed once again in signalling the start of this new uptrend. This is shown in Figure 12.3. In this case the trend is a horizontal channel, one unit in depth, throughout March 1995, and has five troughs and four peaks lying on its boundaries. The RFI broke out of this channel on 23rd March, with the Index at 3135. While this is a

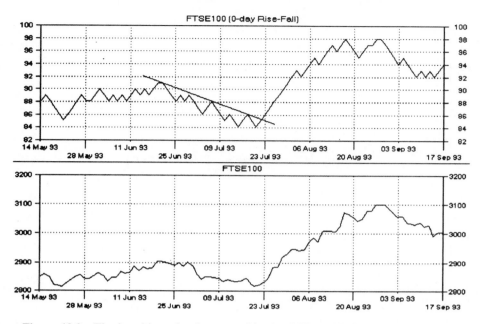

Figure 12.2 The breaking of a downtrend in the RFI on 23rd July 1993 signals the start of a new uptrend in the FTSE100 Index

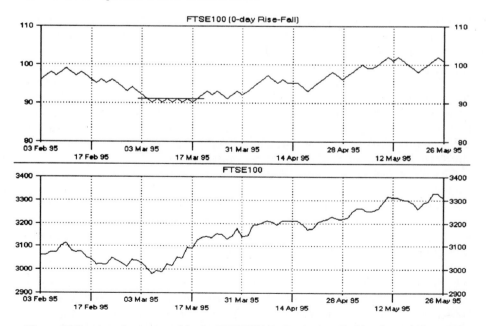

Figure 12.3 Another uptrend in the FTSE100 Index is signalled by the crossing of the horizontal channel in the RFI (upper panel) on 23rd March 1995

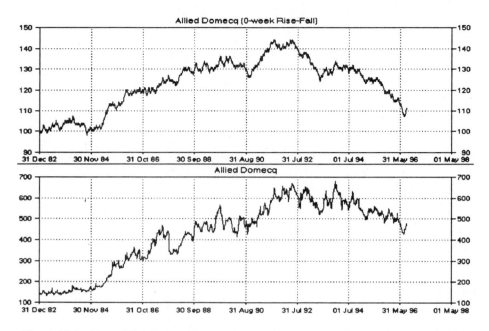

Figure 12.4   The Allied Domecq share price (lower panel) with the RFI (upper panel)

little way above the low point in the Index earlier in March, it was still a
good time at which to make investments, since the Index rose consistently
over the next year to reach just short of 3800.

The general picture of the RFI for Allied Domecq is shown in Figure
12.4. Here weekly data have been used in order to present a longer timescale. Again, most of the major peaks and troughs in the share price have a
counterpart in the RFI. Note that the fall of over 100p during the crash of
October 1987 shows no significant reaction in the RFI. That is because the
RFI can only change by one unit whatever the scale of the rise or fall in the
share price in one day or, in this case, one week.

Figure 12.5 shows the portion of the chart for 1990 to 1991. The downtrend line, when broken in October 1990, would have got the investor into
the share at 464p. Although this is some 40p above the low point of 426p
which occurred a few weeks earlier, i.e. about 10% off the bottom, the
share then made excellent progress over the next two years to take it to the
mid-600p level for a 40% gain over the period.

Figure 12.6 shows how the RFI would have got the investor out of
Allied Domecq following this investment in October 1990. The uptrend
line, with many points lying on it, was broken in September 1991, with the
share price at 610p. Thus, the investor, using just the RFI for this one-year
ride on Allied Domecq, would have seen a gain of 31% in just under one
year. Although the share price subsequently rose to the mid-600p level,

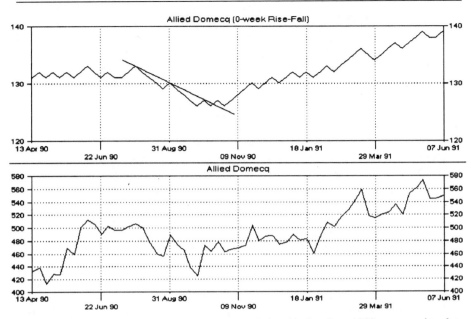

Figure 12.5 The breaking of the downtrend line in October 1990 gave a signal to enter the share at a price of 464p. A good rise to over 600p followed

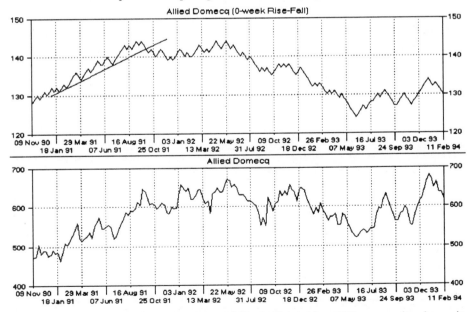

Figure 12.6 The breaking of the uptrend line in September 1991 gave a signal to exit the share at a price of 610p. This kept the investor out of a whole year of sideways movement. The breaking of the downtrend line in July 1993 gave a signal to re-enter the share at a price of 545p

this took until 22nd May 1992. An investor using a stop loss method would probably have sold at about 620p, so that staying in the share once the RFI signalled an exit would have netted only an additional 2.5% over the following eight months. This would hardly be a very profitable use of capital at a time when there would be many better opportunities in other shares.

Also shown in Figure 12.6 is the breaking of the subsequent downtrend in the RFI, giving the investor the opportunity to re-enter the share in July 1993 at a price of around 545p. From this point the price rose quite rapidly to 685p for a very useful gain, but a glance at the chart in Figure 12.4 shows that this was the last real opportunity in Allied Domecq with the share entering a long downtrend from its subsequent peak.

The case of British Steel was discussed in the last chapter as an example where the Welles Wilder Index gave a false buying signal, getting the investor involved at a time when the share price continued to fall. The indicator gave false buying signals on 10th October 1995 at 167.5p and on 3rd November 1995 at 153p. The RFI for this share is shown in Figure 12.7. The downtrend shown in the RFI in October/November 1995 was broken in early November with the price at 157p. Thus this indicator avoids giving a buying signal too early as was the case with the Welles Wilder Index.

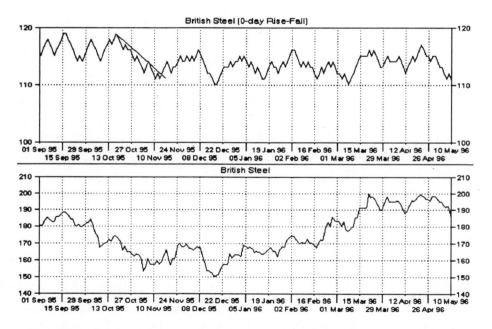

Figure 12.7 The breaking of the downtrend line in the RFI in November 1995 gave a buying signal for British Steel

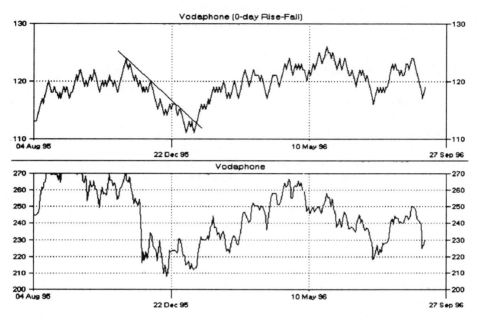

Figure 12.8 The Vodaphone share price. The downtrend in the RFI was broken in January 1996

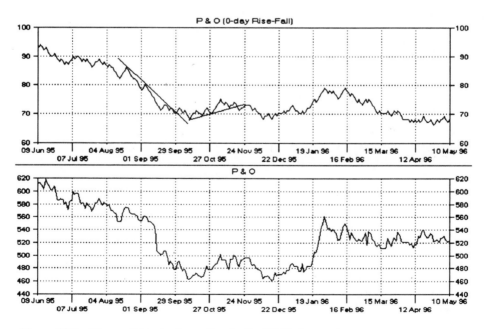

Figure 12.9 The earthquake formation in the P&O share price

Vodaphone (Figure 12.8) is another share in which the breaking of a downtrend by the RFI gave a good buying signal. There are four peaks touching the downtrend line shown in Figure 12.8, and the RFI broke up through this line on 15th January 1996 with the share price at 211.5p. This was the start of a useful rise in the share price, which reached 265.5p by 30th April 1996 for a 25% gain in just over three months.

As a final example, we showed in Chapter 11 how the earthquake formation in the P&O share price caused a difficulty with other indicators due to the rapid change in the share price. In Figure 12.9 is shown the RFI for this period of time. In this case the downtrend was broken on 29th September 1995 with the share price at 478p, i.e. nearly at the bottom of the fall. As can be seen, the following uptrend was broken on 20th November 1995 at 486p, before the price rose up on the other side of the formation.

The investor would therefore have suffered a small loss over the course of two months, and would not have been left in the share to enjoy the rise to the 560p level. Thus, as with other indicators, the RFI is usually not able to deal with rapid movements of this type.

Although, as we have shown, there are occasions where the RFI method generates late selling signals, it is much more useful as a generator of buying signals, and the examples given in this chapter should serve to illustrate the power of this indicator.

13

Channel Analysis

The 'envelope method' was first described by J.M. Hurst in the United States in 1970 and has since been developed in the UK into the technique now known as Channel Analysis (CA). The name is derived from the fact that share prices can be shown to remain within channels of constant depth, and a fairly simple analysis of the share price data will provide all of the information necessary to draw these channels.

The CA technique is an extremely powerful method for determining the most probable course of the share price over the near future, taking into account the degree of randomness inherent in share price movement. It will alert the investor to the probability that a trend in the share price will change direction within this future time window, so that the investor is well placed to take advantage of the change once it has been confirmed.

Note the above emphasis on confirmation that a change in direction has occurred. CA is a probability based method that takes into account the cyclical predictable components and the unpredictable random components of share prices. CA therefore signals that it is *highly probable* that a trend will change direction at a certain point in the near future, but there is still a finite possibility that the direction will change sooner or later than this. The Gulf crisis is a prime example of an unforeseen random event with a particularly depressing effect on world stock markets. Waiting for confirmation of a predicted change will prevent the investor from jumping in too soon and be carried along in the wrong direction by an adverse trend that seems never-ending.

The use of terms such as 'probability based', 'predictable cyclical components' and the like may give the impression that a degree in mathematics or statistics is necessary before an investor can begin to understand or take advantage of channel analysis. Nothing could be further from the truth, since excellent results can be obtained with nothing more than a chart of a share price and a pencil. In other words, channel analysis is an ideal technique for those investors who are inclined towards charting methods in general.

The guiding principles of the CA technique can be encapsulated in a number of observations:

- Share price movement contains both random and cyclical components.
- A channel of constant depth can be drawn so that the share price will penetrate the channel boundaries on only a few occasions. The depth should be the minimum possible commensurate with the restriction on boundary penetration.
- The channel can be projected a limited distance into the future. Future price movement will obey the same rules as past movement, i.e. the vast majority of the movement will be contained within the channel.
- When the share price approaches the upper or lower boundary of the channel, there is a high probability that it will reverse direction.
- The shape of the channel is due to cycles, i.e. trends, in the share price of periodicity greater than the periodicity of the channel.
- The price movement within the channel is due to random movement and the effect of cycles, i.e. trends, of periodicity equal to or less than that of the channel itself.
- Further channels can be constructed outside existing channels. The rule then is that the outer channel should be constructed with the minimum depth possible subject to the restriction that the inner channel should not penetrate the outer channel substantially.
- The advantage of using several channels nested within each other is that they can be drawn so as to represent short term, medium term and long term trends. The investor will then be able to estimate for how long a particular trend will persist before it is forced to change direction by a more dominant longer term trend.

With a computer system these channels will be drawn automatically such as to obey the rules for penetration by prices and other channels, and the figures in this chapter are produced in this way by the Microvest 5.0 package. It should be noted that many computer packages that draw 'envelopes' are not drawing channels in the way that they should be drawn. Many use a constant percentage from the central average rather than a constant depth, and many use a fixed number of standard deviations from the central average. While these may have their uses, they are not based on the vital concept of adjusting boundaries so that only a small percentage of data points lie outside them.

For the pencil and paper investor, it will be found that only a small amount of practice is necessary in order that channels can be drawn by eye with a high degree of accuracy.

Some shares are much more amenable to CA than others. High volatility is a prime requirement, since the better timing of the investment imposed by CA will enable the investor to take advantage of a large proportion of the rises. In this context it should be noted that high volatility should apply to short term movements as well as long term ones.

A useful starting point for a discussion of the power of channel analysis is the Allied Domecq share price. Figure 13.1 shows nearly 14 years of weekly data with a channel of constant depth drawn so as to contain the short term price movements. There are at least 20 occasions when the price is at the upper boundary for a short period of time, and a similar number for the lower boundary. The channel has been drawn in this case so that only 3.5% of points lie outside the boundary. It follows that if the share price is currently at or just outside a boundary, then the probability of it staying in that position is small. A close inspection of Figure 13.1 shows that when the price rebounds from a boundary, it eventually reaches the opposite boundary. The vertical channel depth in this instance is about 100p. When the price rises from the lower boundary to the upper one, the change would be 100p for a horizontal channel, more than this if the channel is rising (the amount by which the channel has risen has to be added to the 100p), and less than this if the channel is falling (the amount by which the channel has fallen has to be deducted from the 100p).

We can see now how CA provides a great advantage over the other type of indicator discussed in this book: not only can we determine when a price trend is likely to change direction by virtue of it being at a boundary, but we can estimate a target area into which the price should eventually arrive, i.e. quantify the extent of the trend that we are using for our investment.

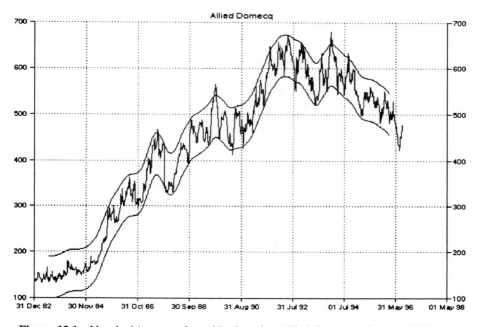

Figure 13.1 Nearly 14 years of weekly data for Allied Domecq show that the short term price movements are contained within a constant depth channel which is drawn around the Allied Domecq share price

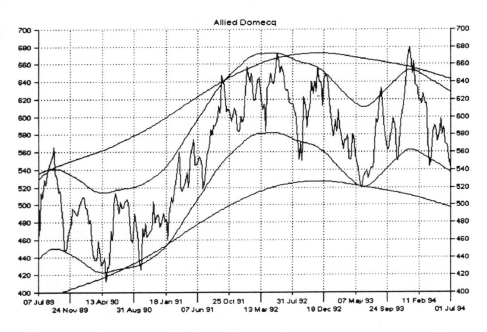

Figure 13.2 A shorter section of the Allied Domecq price history using a 53-week and a 201-week channel

A much better appreciation of the way the price oscillates inside the inner channel and the way in which the inner channel oscillates within the outer channel can be obtained from the enlarged part of the chart shown in Figure 13.2. Two channels are now drawn, the inner one being based on a 53-week average and the outer one on a 201-week average, for a five-year section of the data. Here we can see that there are 10 points where the price touches or crosses the lower boundary of the inner channel, and 10 points where it touches or crosses the upper boundary of the inner channel.

There are also three places where the inner channel is at or slightly above the upper boundary of the outer channel, and two places where the inner channel is at or slightly below the lower boundary of the outer channel.

While the channel in Figure 13.1 had a depth of approximately 100p, the better detail of Figure 13.2 enables us to see that the inner channel (the same as was drawn in Figure 13.1) has a depth of 92p, while the outer one, not drawn in Figure 13.1, has a depth of 140p. Channel depth is a function of the average upon which the channel is based when drawn by computer. The longer the span of the average, the greater is the channel depth. The value of the average is chosen for the reasons discussed in Chapter 10 on moving averages, i.e. to remove trends of shorter periodicity than the ones we are interested in. In Figure 13.2, therefore, values of 53 weeks and 201 weeks have been chosen in order to focus on fluctuations of greater than one year and greater than about four years. Thus we expect troughs in the inner channel to occur more than one year apart, and peaks to occur more than one year apart. It follows that the gap between a trough and a peak, i.e. the points at which the inner channel touches the lower boundary and then the upper boundary of the outer channel, will be at least six months. This is a useful period to allow for the payoff from the initial investment. Similarly, peaks and troughs in the outer channel will be at least two years apart. However, the outer channels in this and succeeding charts are not used primarily in the sense of estimating when they turn, but rather in providing a boundary against which the inner channel will bounce. The smoother nature of the outer channel makes it easier to extrapolate it into the future. Since the channels are based on centred moving averages, the turning points in them will not become obvious until a point in time half a span of the average after the turning point. Thus it is at channel turning points that difficulty will arise, since the extrapolation of the previous direction of the channel will show it going in the wrong direction. It is for this reason that investors should wait until various indications are being given that the channel has changed direction before an investment is made. Such reasoning is employed in the next example to determine that a channel must have changed direction.

The section of the Allied Domecq share price from October 1988 to early 1991 is shown in Figure 13.3. Up to the low point at the end of April 1990 the outer channel was falling, although the rate of fall was declining. The event that confirmed that the outer channel must have changed direction from April onwards is the almost vertical rise to the peak at 518p. If the outer channel had been extrapolated so as to continue downwards then this peak would have violated the upper boundary by a very large amount. The only way in which this peak can lie close to the upper boundary is if the outer channel has turned up prior to that point.

This bend in the outer channel must be accompanied by a change in the direction of the inner channel so that it, too, is rising after the low point in April 1990. Since the price is at the top of both inner and outer channels when at the peak price of 518p, this is not the time to buy. From that point onwards the inner channel has bounced back from the upper boundary of the outer channel and is then falling. Although the price falls to the bottom of this inner channel in August 1990, this would not be a good time to buy since this channel is falling. The optimum time is when both channels are rising, and this occurs when the price drops rapidly from 488p to 425p. At this level the price is at the extrapolated lower boundary, and therefore must be expected to bounce back. Since the extrapolated direction of the outer channel is upwards, the inner channel must bounce upwards from it, so that following this trough we have the desired situation that both channels are rising.

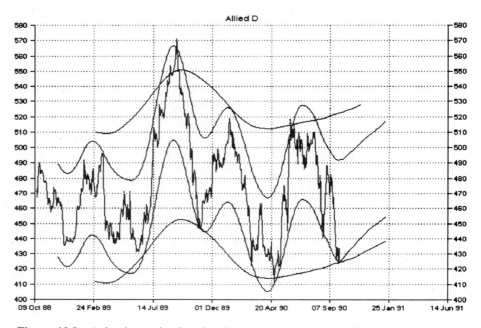

Figure 13.3 A buying point has just been reached in September 1990 for Allied Domecq

We must wait for the price to form a trough at the lower boundaries, since the random content of price movement may cause the price to fall below the lower channel boundary. As can be seen on closer inspection, the price actually forms two troughs at the boundary. An investor buying after the first one would be paying 434p for the share, and would see the price fall back to 425p before recovering back to 434p. Since this fall to 425p is only just over 2%, a stop loss would not be triggered. The investor would then be able to take advantage of a very rapid rise in price to 485p, i.e. 11% in a matter of a few days.

This subsequent movement of the price can be seen in Figure 13.4. The level of 485p, rapidly reached, is still below the extrapolated upper boundary of the inner channel as well as being only just over halfway up from the lower boundary of the outer channel. Thus the investor would not envisage selling at this point since the target area at the upper boundary has not been reached. However, a stop loss would be in operation at all times to cover those cases where the price falls back without ever reaching the upper boundary. Although the price then dips from this peak of 485p, it falls exactly 5%, so would not trigger a stop loss of 5%, which requires this percentage to be exceeded.

A few weeks later, the price has risen again to 505p. As shown in Figure 13.4, this is now at the upper boundary of the inner channel, even though

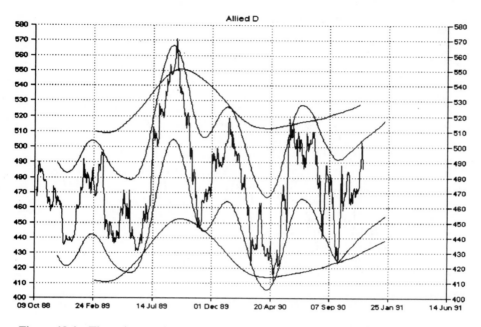

Figure 13.4 The price reached the upper boundary of the inner channel at 505p, thus reaching the selling area

the inner channel has not reached the top of the outer one. Thus the probability of the price falling back from this level is high. The investor now has two courses of action: firstly, to sell on the grounds that since the price will probably fall, it is best to leave the share; or secondly, to stay with it since the inner channel is still rising and has yet to meet the upper boundary of the outer channel so that a price fall would be only temporary.

The investor taking the first course of action would probably achieve a price of 488p in view of the rapid retreat from the peak price of 505p. From this one buying and selling operation, the investor would have made a gain of 12% in just over two months.

The investor who sold would have another opportunity to get back on board once the price reached the lower boundary again on 25th January 1991. The trough price was 461p, but since a rise from this low point is necessary in order to define the trough, the buying point would come the next day at a price of 472p, i.e. at a price some 16p lower than the price he sold for a few weeks previously. This point can be seen in Figure 13.5.

Figure 13.5 also shows the price entering the selling area with the sharp rise to 568p. At this point the price is at the smoothest extrapolation of the upper boundaries of both the inner and outer channels. This is now a strong selling indication since it is clear that the inner channel is about to

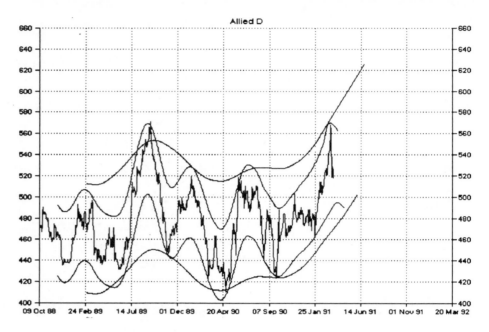

Figure 13.5   There was another buying opportunity in January 1991 once the price rose from the trough of 462p. The price then enters the selling area at the upper boundaries at around 568p

bounce downwards from the outer channel boundary. As with all channel selling signals, the investor must wait for a peak to be formed, so must suffer a fall from the peak value, even though occasionally this might be a rapid fall. In the present case, the price drops to 539p, which is the signal to exit the share for another useful profit. The investor who stayed in from 434p would see a 24% gain, while the investor who bought at 472p would see a 14% gain.

In Figure 13.6 we can see that there was yet another opportunity in Allied Domecq, with the price having fallen rapidly back to just above 500p. At this point, the projected inner channel would still be rising, as would the outer channel. Since this new low point would be on the lower boundary of the inner channel, the rise from this low point would signal a buy. The corresponding selling signal would occur in the group of peaks at around 570p, giving a rise of the order of 65p.

Figure 13.6 also shows the next buying point, with the price down to 520p. At this point the inner channel must have fallen from the high point around the 580p level, and would meet the rising lower boundary of the outer channel, to give a bounce back upwards. The investor, waiting for the rise from 520p to define the trough, would be able to buy at about 522p, since the price stayed at that point for a few days. Figure 13.7 shows

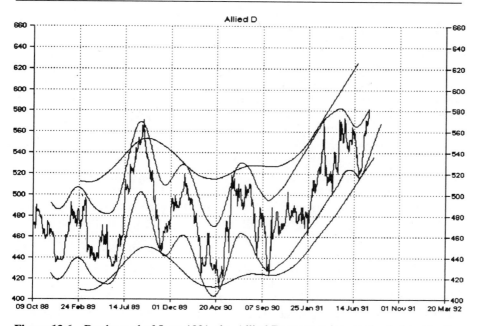

Figure 13.6 By the end of June 1991, the Allied Domecq price was back down to the extrapolated lower boundary of the outer channel, providing another buying opportunity at about 525p

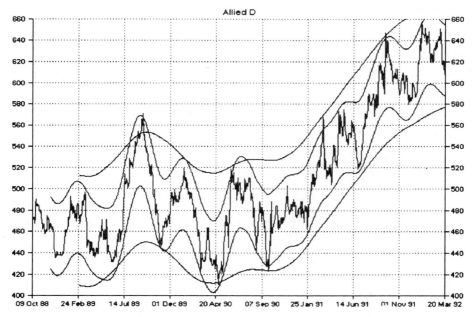

Figure 13.7 The actual channels produced by computer subsequent to the price movements discussed previously show how accurate the predictions were

the subsequent course of the price and channels as produced by computer some time in the future, showing that the projections and predictions of turning points were extremely accurate.

It is interesting to note the behaviour of the inner channel when viewed over a long timescale such as that in Figure 13.7. From October 1988 to September 1990 the channel exhibited marked cyclical behaviour. This disappeared from then until June 1991 when it reappeared again. As mentioned in the next chapter, this is a characteristic of cyclic behaviour in the stock market; it waxes and wanes periodically in an unpredictable fashion. Shares which are just entering a phase where a cycle of particular nominal wavelength is becoming important are likely to maintain this particular cycle for some time, whereas shares which have been in such a phase for some time are likely to see this cycle disappear for some time. Although sometimes a cycle of a certain nominal wavelength may fluctuate in a similar fashion in many shares at the same time, this may not always be the case. This is shown by the example of Glynwed, in Figure 13.8. As with Allied Domecq, the cyclical behaviour of the inner channel is quite marked for at least two years, but then disappears in July 1992, the inner channel then being really a version of the outer channel but with less depth. However, Glynwed and Allied Domecq went through their marked cyclical behaviour at totally different times.

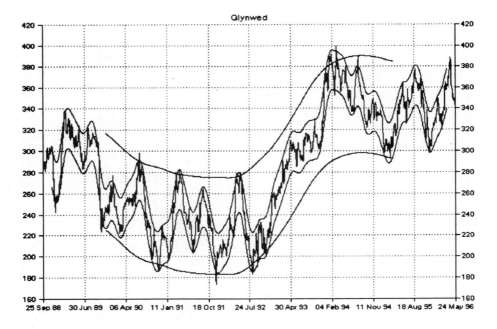

Figure 13.8 Channels in the Glynwed share price. Note how the inner channel is very sinusoidal for two years, but that the amplitude of this cycle disappears in July 1992

Although well-defined cycles of large amplitude for the inner channel have the advantage that the buying and selling points will be extremely well defined, there is an obvious disadvantage in that the investor is buying and selling at frequent intervals. This can often mean that a long term uptrend in the share price can see the investor making several forays into the same share, whereas he would have been more comfortable with buying and riding the uptrend for a longer period.

The Glynwed example is a good one of the disappearance of the fluctuations in the inner channel allowing the investor to stay on board for a very long and sustained rise. The decision-making process by which the investor bought in August 1992 can be explained by reference to Figure 13.9, where the channels as they would be interpreted at that time are shown.

The lowest point in the share price was reached on 5th December 1991 at 173p. At that point, the outer channel would be extrapolated as still falling, with a depth of 90p. The feature that determines that the outer channel must have turned upwards is the twin peak formation on 24th April 1992 at 279p and 22nd May 1992 at 278p. To maintain a channel depth of 90p would mean that the lower boundary must be 90p below these peaks at 278/279p, i.e. at 188 or 189p. However, if the outer channel had continued in its falling mode then the lower boundary would lie at a level of about 170p, some 18p or 19p lower than calculated. The only way

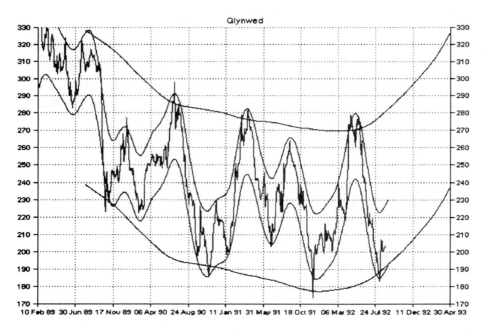

Figure 13.9 A buying point in August 1992 in Glynwed. The price is just up from the extrapolated position of the lower boundary of the outer channel

the lower boundary can be made to pass through or close to 189p is by bending it upwards, i.e. taking the low point of 173p in December 1991 as the turning point.

Now that we have deduced that we have an upward trending outer channel, the buying point will be given when the price, contained within the short term channel, falls to this rising lower boundary. This happens with a fall to 183p on 13th August 1992. The investor must wait of course for the price to rise from that point in order to establish that a trough was formed at or near to the boundary. This happens when the price rises to 196p the next day. Thus everything is pointing to a good potential for the share price: this outer channel is rising, but has not been rising for long, and the inner channel which was falling must be about to bounce upwards from it. Thus the investor can buy with confidence.

As can be seen from the previous figure, this was a marvellous buying opportunity, since the price rose without triggering a stop loss or reaching the top of the extrapolated channel until February 1994. The price at that time was round 390p, giving the investor a near 100% profit.

Although these examples show the power of the method, it is still vulnerable to the unexpected random movement that no indicator can cope with. There will be occasions when a channel, having just changed direction for the better, reverses direction some weeks later without running the expected profitable course.

Adverse and totally unpredictable movements such as these, soon after a buying operation has been carried out, can easily be protected against by a stop loss which is geared to the channel analysis technique. This is readily done by keeping a level a few percent below the predicted lower boundary of the inner channel. Then as soon as the price falls down through the projected channel and reaches the rising stop loss level, the share should be sold. Such an approach will limit the damage caused to just a few percent, and this will easily be recovered by the subsequent profitable investments.

14

Cycles and Probability

Although the charts shown in this book so far have been produced by computer, they could just as well have been produced by manual plotting on graph paper. Many of the indicators consist of trendlines, which could be drawn on the chart by means of a ruler or flexible curve. Other indicators such as moving averages, Welles Wilder, Relative Strength and the Rise–Fall Indicator require a fairly simple calculation, which although perhaps tedious, could be carried out with the aid of a calculator.

While computers obviously speed up the process of producing a chart and carrying out these types of calculations, a few computer packages are now taking advantage of the power of computers to carry out tasks which are so complex that they are impossible to do in any other way. The analysis of cycles present in stock market data, and the determination of the probability associated with the change in direction of a long term trend, are good examples of the application of computers to develop new fields of research.

CYCLES IN STOCK MARKET DATA

An analysis of stock market data by mathematical techniques such as Fourier Analysis shows that all possible wavelengths from one day to many years are present in the data. However, fortunately, some wavelengths are much more dominant than others, so that the possibility exists of using important wavelengths present in the data to fine tune an investment decision. A package such as Microvest 5.0 is able to highlight a narrow window around a specified wavelength, and display this along with the original data. An example is shown in Figure 14.1 for Allied Domecq. Here the nominal one-year (261-day) cycle has been extracted from the data. In Figure 14.2 the nominal 25-day cycle has been extracted. A number of observations can be made from these two figures:

- The wavelength, i.e. peak to peak distance, is not an exact, constant 261 or 25 days, but varies either side of these values. This is why the term 'nominal' is used to describe it.
- The amplitude, i.e. trough to adjacent peak distance, also varies considerably.
- The nominal cycle passes through phases of strongly ordered cyclicality followed by phases of disorder in which amplitude and wavelength are unpredictable.

The first two of these observations mean that cycles normally have a high degree of predictability, since if wavelength and amplitude are varying within certain limits, then the behaviour of the cycle in the immediate future can be predicted within such limits. This would lead to predictions that a cycle has probably just bottomed out, and will probably rise by such and such an amount before topping out again at a certain point in the future within a window of plus or minus *x* days or weeks. While this statement is obviously hedged with ifs and buts, the fact is that the limits to be applied to the prediction are not that wide, and therefore give a good indication of the future behaviour.

It is the third observation that can cause a difficulty. What was a good prediction of future behaviour can go haywire because the cycle being observed is just about to disappear for a while, i.e. the ever-present threat

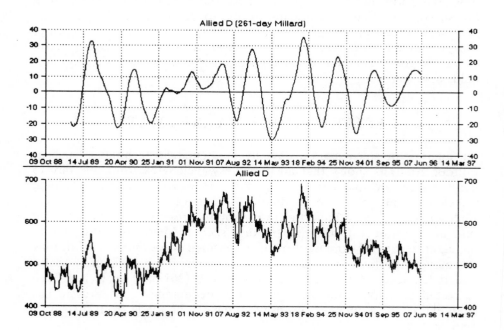

Figure 14.1   The upper panel shows the nominal 261-day cycle in Allied Domecq

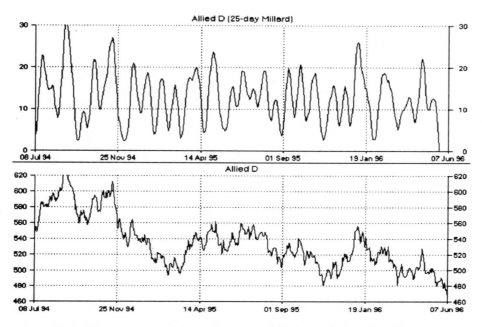

Figure 14.2 The upper panel shows the nominal 25-day cycle in Allied Domecq

of random behaviour strikes out of the blue. Fortunately, this random behaviour of a nominal cycle persists for only about a quarter to a third of the time as can be demonstrated when long price histories are analysed. This means that as long as the possibility of a reversion to random behaviour is constantly borne in mind, cycle analysis is an extremely powerful technique for predicting future behaviour.

At this point, it is important to make the link between the behaviour of a cycle and the behaviour of the share price. We have already commented that some cycles are very important while others are not. In Figure 14.1 we can see that between August 1992 and February 1994 the 261-day cycle had a maximum amplitude of the order of 65p, i.e. swinging from –30 to +35. This is the contribution that the cycle makes to the share price, i.e. it caused a 65p increase in the share price. It can be seen that the low in the cycle is exactly lined up with the low point in the share price. Thus a correct prediction of the state of the cycle would have got the investor into the share at this low point to enjoy a substantial rise. The rise is more than the 65p caused by the 261-day cycle because it is probable that many other cycles also bottomed out at the same time, adding their contribution to the rise in the share price.

The point has to be made here that the mathematics of cycle analysis means that the last section of the cycle has to be estimated using probability techniques, i.e. the current status of a cycle is not known exactly but is a best estimate.

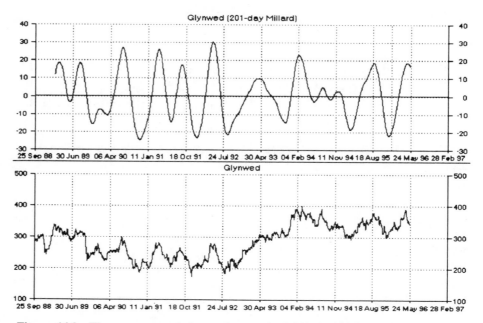

Figure 14.3 The upper panel shows the nominal 201-day cycle in Glynwed. This shows that regular behaviour disappeared temporarily in July 1992, as was noted in the channel analysis example in the last chapter

We noted in the last chapter that the channels drawn for Glynwed showed a cyclical behaviour of the inner channel which then disappeared when the price entered its long uptrend. An analysis of the 201-day cycle in Glynwed (Figure 14.3) now confirms that the cyclicality did indeed become random in July 1992 for a period.

As an example of the application of cycle analysis to decision making, we can take the example of Glynwed as already discussed in the last chapter. We noted that the low point in the price occurred on 5th December 1991 at 173p. Channel analysis would not have allowed us to buy since the prediction at that time was that the outer channel was still falling. In Figure 14.4 we show the predicted status of the 201-day cycle a few days later once the price had risen from the low. The prediction is that the cycle has only just passed its peak, and is therefore on its way down. Obviously at this point no investment would be made, since the falling cycle would have a negative effect on the share price.

The channel analysis of Glynwed in the last chapter showed that an investment would have been made on 17th August 1992 with the price at 207p, because the price had just rebounded from the extrapolated lower boundary of the channel. Figure 14.5 shows the predicted status of the 201-day cycle at that time. The cycle is rapidly approaching its trough, so that it

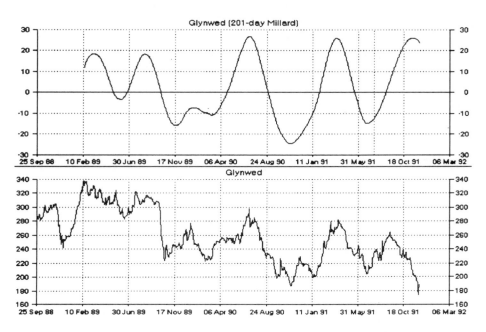

Figure 14.4 The upper panel shows the nominal 201-day cycle in Glynwed. At the time the price moved up from the low point of 173p on 5th December 1991, the prediction for the 201-day cycle is that it has just topped out. No investment would be made

is expected to turn up shortly. It is probably nearer the turn than is shown in the figure for the reason that the predicted peak is somewhat delayed in time compared with the group of peaks in the share price. Since normally the peak of the cycle should correspond in time to important peaks in the share price, then the estimation of the trough in the cycle is probably running a number of days late.

Assistance in this matter can be obtained from a view of a cycle of shorter wavelength. Figure 14.6 shows the 101-day cycle in Glynwed. Here we can see that this particular cycle has bottomed out, and is on its way up. As further confirmation that a number of important cycles are bottoming out at this point, the predicted status of the 25-day cycle is shown in Figure 14.7. Again, this cycle has just bottomed out.

Taking into account therefore that two major cycles have just bottomed out and that the 201-day cycle is rapidly approaching its bottom, the investment in Glynwed based on channel analysis is therefore confirmed. We noted in the last chapter that a large rise followed from this point, with the price reaching 400p from this buying level of 207p. This large rise is due to the fact that many cycles had reached their turning points at the same time, and since their effect is additive, a healthy rise was to be anticipated.

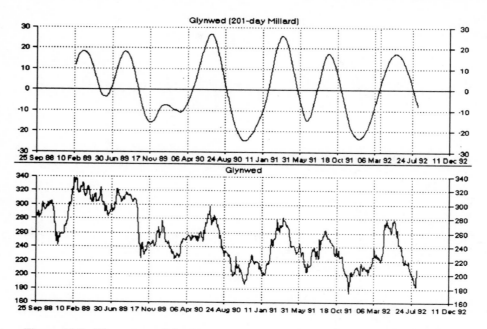

Figure 14.5 The status of the 201-day cycle in Glynwed on 17th August 1992. The turning point will be arriving soon

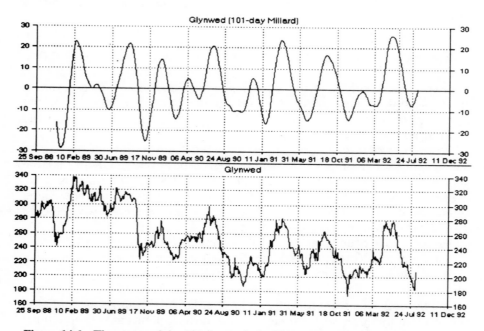

Figure 14.6 The status of the 101-day cycle in Glynwed on 17 August 1992

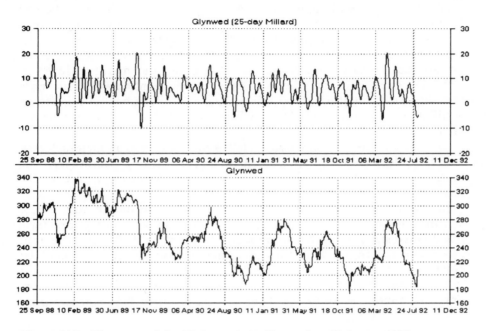

Figure 14.7 The status of the 25-day cycle in Glynwed on 17 August 1992

As a general rule, a number of cycles should be examined routinely in this way in order to determine such 'golden points' where the majority of them are bottoming out or about to bottom out. Looking back historically at such golden points, an interesting observation is that it often appears that the various nominal cycles which will coincide at the golden point begin to change their wavelengths some time in advance so that this coincidence will occur.

TURNING POINT PROBABILITY

The analysis of cycles in stock market data is taken a great deal further by the Sigma-p probability program. It is only the availability of faster microcomputers that has enabled the complex calculations of multiple cycles and the application of probability and chaos theory to be applied to stock market data. The extensive mathematics used in such calculations have now pushed out the frontiers of predictability to about a year into the future. Naturally, the considerable random content present in cyclical behaviour has to be kept in mind, so that such a program is best operated alongside a stop loss so that the investor is protected as far as possible against a random termination of a predicted trend.

An example is shown in Figure 14.8. The program is asked to predict, on 12th October 1990, at what point the long term trend might have changed direction, and when it would change direction again. As can be seen, the chevrons indicate these turning points, and on 12th October show that the uptrend has already been in existence for about four months. However, with the price comfortably below 500p, an investment can be made since the prediction is that the trend will continue until October 1991, i.e. there is still another year to go before the investment will be in the termination area.

The validity of the prediction is shown one year later in October 1991, with the price now having peaked at 645p (Figure 14.9). An investor who bought a year earlier at 485p would therefore see a 32% gain over the year.

In another example, the prediction made for Boots on 4th May 1990 is shown in Figure 14.10. The most probable turning point in the long term trend was estimated to be around 21st September 1990, i.e. some four months in the future. The turn after that was predicted at around 1st November 1991.

The accuracy of the prediction is shown by the view of the subsequent price movement as shown in Figure 14.11. As can be seen, the price

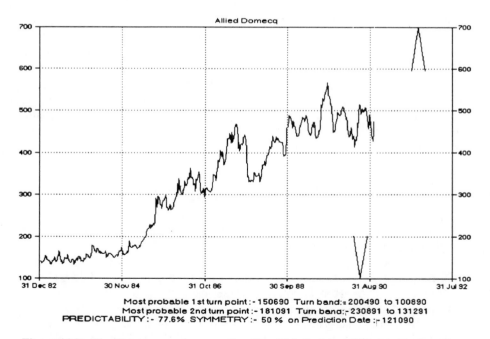

Most probable 1st turn point :- 150690 Turn band:= 200490 to 100890
Most probable 2nd turn point :- 181091 Turn band:- 230891 to 131291
PREDICTABILITY :- 77.6% SYMMETRY :- 50 % on Prediction Date :- 121090

Figure 14.8 The Sigma-p program predicted on 12th October 1990 that the long term trend in Allied Domecq had already turned up and would peak around the end of October 1991, i.e. would last about a year

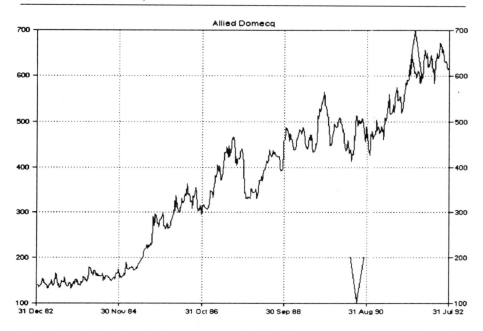

Figure 14.9 This view of price movement in Allied Domecq up to July 1992 shows the accuracy of the Sigma-p prediction made in October 1990

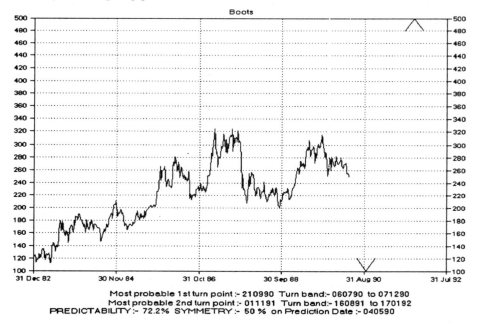

Most probable 1st turn point :- 210990 Turn band:- 060790 to 071290
Most probable 2nd turn point :- 011191 Turn band:- 160891 to 170192
PREDICTABILITY :- 72.2% SYMMETRY :- 50 % on Prediction Date :- 040590

Figure 14.10 The Sigma-p program predicted on 4th May 1990 that the long term trend in Boots would turn up around the end of September 1990 and would run until November 1991

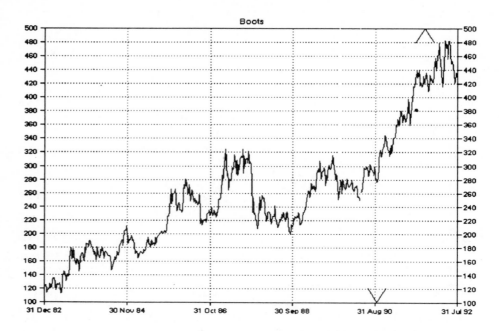

Figure 14.11 This view of price movement in Boots up to July 1992 shows the accuracy of the Sigma-p prediction made over a year earlier

enjoyed a long run up to 480p over the next year, giving the investor a handsome profit.

The last chapter, on channel analysis, showed that there was always a problem at channel turning points when the channels were extrapolated, since the extrapolation would show channels continuing in the wrong direction until the data reached a point about half a span of the average after the turn. The Sigma-p program, since it is based on probabilities, provides much better estimates of channel turning points than those produced by extrapolation, as can be seen from the chart of Boots in Figure 14.12. At the time of the prediction in May 1995, i.e. where the channels terminate, the normal extrapolation shows the channel to be still falling, even though the subsequent data shown in the figure mean that the channel must have changed direction. The probability estimate shows the channel to have changed direction around the end of January 1995, so that an investment could now be made, thus taking advantage of a very good rise to the 600p level in early 1996.

The examples in this chapter are meant to give the reader a flavour of the important contribution that computers are making and will make in the future in the field of investment research. It must be stressed again, as it has been throughout this book, that share prices are subject to random

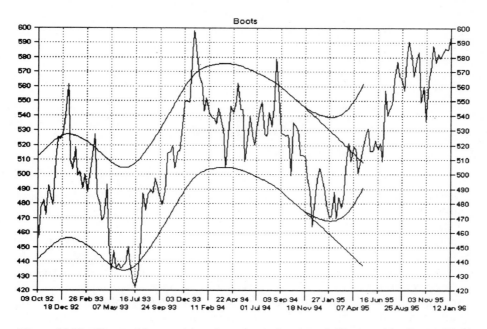

Figure 14.12 The problem at channel turning points is well illustrated for Boots. The downward trending channel is the result of the usual channel extrapolation method, and from the future price movement can be seen to be incorrect. The upward turning, correct channel is produced from a probability analysis by Sigma-p

influences. Because they are random, it makes no difference how powerful the computer or computer program is that is being used to predict prices, there will never be such a thing as a cast-iron prediction.

15

Conclusion

The following rules were first put forward in the book *Channel Analysis*, and have been modified slightly because of the differing subject matter of this book.

The main way in which investors lose money is to fail to admit that they have made a mistake, and thereby fail to cut short a losing position early on before substantial losses have accumulated. If investors can overcome this psychological problem, they shift the balance of probabilities even more in their favour, because they will allow their profits to run while minimising their losses. Failure to maintain discipline at all times will totally negate the powerful techniques which have been presented in this book. Some guideline rules which should help the investor to maintain this discipline are presented in the following pages.

CAPITAL MUST BE PRESERVED AT ALL COSTS

This is the first and overriding rule of stock market investment, and the remaining rules and comments are designed so that this first rule can be followed consistently. The natural consequence of this rule is that when a position has been taken in a share, the investor must get out as soon as it is obvious that the share price is misbehaving. There will always be another opportunity for making profit. The prevention of loss is as important as the achievement of profit. Remember there is no such thing as a paper loss. All losses are real.

NEVER ACT SOLELY ON ADVICE

Besides the internal pressure to stray from this disciplined path caused by investor psychology, the external pressures from the investment industry are immense. The investor is constantly bombarded with advice from stockbrokers, junk mail and the media. Some of the most successful investors read nothing but the share prices page in their newspaper and do not even glance at the rest of the business section. I would not go quite as far as this, since a feel for the general investment climate which can be gained from these pages can be extremely valuable. By all means listen to advice from whatever source, but never, never, act on it without analysing the data by the methods discussed in this book and then act only if the analysis is favourable.

NEVER PUT MORE THAN ONE-EIGHTH OF YOUR CAPITAL IN ONE SHARE

However positively the investor feels about the potential for a particular share, this positive feeling must be tempered by knowledge of the existence of random movement. Because of this, the investor should not, and must not, have 100% confidence in any one given situation. The temptation to go for broke and put everything into one magic share is always at the back of the investor's mind, and that is where it should stay. Never, never, commit more than one-eighth of the investment capital to one share. This will keep the risk as low as possible while maintaining the potential for profit. From time to time there will be occasions when it is not possible to find eight shares in which to invest. In such cases put the money into short term interest-bearing accounts where it can be got at instantly when the need arises.

DO NOT ANTICIPATE SHARE PRICE TURNING POINTS

Never make an investment until after the change in direction of the trend has been confirmed, and never disinvest until the change in direction has been confirmed. The profit available in upward trends which one buys into shortly after the start of these new trends is such that one does not need to worry about squeezing out an extra one or two percentage points by trying to anticipate them.

PROTECT PROFITS BY STOP LOSSES

Just as it is not necessary to try to squeeze extra gain out of a trend by jumping the gun, so it is not necessary to try to squeeze extra gain by continuing to run after the finishing tape has been passed. In the majority of cases, the termination of an upward trend results in a sudden sharp reversal of price over the course of one or two days. The risk increases dramatically as the inner channel increases in upward slope. Although I have shown by channel analysis that one can determine the selling point closely in time, it is essential to protect oneself against the conjunction of an adverse random movement and a change in direction of short term cycles. This can only be done by using one of the various stop loss methods discussed in Chapter 1. It is better to sell prematurely than to lose profit by staying invested too long in a share which is reaching its peak price.

PROTECT AGAINST LOSSES BY STOP LOSSES

This would appear to mean the same as the previous heading, but here the stop loss is meant to apply not to the profitable position above, but to the case where an incorrect buying decision has been made and the share starts to fall in price instead of rising. In this case the position never was in profit. Even so, the rule about protection of capital is paramount. The temptation is to think that one was slightly premature in recognising the start of the upward trend, and that in a few more days or weeks the expected trend will materialise. This attitude is a major cause of stock market losses, and must never be adopted. Never forget that if you can reduce your losses to say 4–5%, including dealing costs, when you make a bad decision, then this is only 4–5% of one-eighth of your total capital. You could afford to experience theoretically 20 or 25 such losses before one-eighth of your capital was wiped out, and 160–200 such losses before all capital is lost. The chances of such a thing happening are at vanishing point for the conservative investment policy advocated in this book.

STAY WITH FTSE100 AND MID-250 SHARES

The influence of dealing costs on profit is quite large when compounded over a number of transactions. The spread of prices, i.e. the difference between buying and selling prices for a share, is part of this equation. The spread is at a minimum for the top 350 shares, and there is usually plenty of opportunity for finding a share amongst these shares which is approaching an upward trend. If not, then of course move down the capitalisation league table, but accept the fact that the spread will be greater.

IGNORE DIVIDENDS

Dividends are nice to receive, and if the investor is fully invested in eight different shares for most of the year, he can expect to receive many dividends which will add to his profit. That is all that can be said about them, for the investor should never let an impending dividend affect his buying or selling operation. In other words, if the signal comes to sell, do not think of hanging on for a little longer because the dividend will be announced the following week. If a buying point is approaching, do not buy in before the change in direction is confirmed simply because a dividend will be captured.

KEEP TRACK OF THE MARKET

It is always essential that the general investment climate is tracked by means of a market indicator such as the FT All Share Index or the FTSE100 Index. Weekly values are sufficient to do this. In spite of recent speculation that the London market is becoming uncoupled from Wall Street, short term dramatic movements in the US market almost always affect the London market. Thus it is a good idea to keep track of the Dow Jones Index on a weekly basis.

If the market is falling, adopt a more cautious stance towards your existing holdings and new purchases, and watch your stop losses very carefully. The investor may well find that in the initial stages it is very difficult to stick to this investment philosophy. He may find that straying off this narrow path brings him an instant reward that he would otherwise have missed. This is just the quixotic nature of the world of probability. Over a number of years the investor following these guidelines will see his capital gaining steadily in value, while the investor who allows himself to be diverted from time to time will be subjecting himself to increasing risk that will inevitably take its toll. Finally, the investor who has successfully followed these techniques for perhaps a year or so will begin to look for greater gains than those which can be made out of investment in shares. Then, and not before, is the time to turn to the magnifying effect of dealing in traded options. In inexperienced hands traded options can be unacceptably risky, but they can be extremely rewarding when they are thoroughly understood and when the investor is correct about the movement of the underlying security. The author's book *Traded Options Simplified* (see Appendix) will take the beginner from the basics through to simple strategies and then on to advanced strategies, as well as discussing some powerful new techniques for investors familiar with the field.

Appendix

Addresses

For lists of brokers: The Secretary, The International Stock Exchange of the United Kingdom and the Republic of Ireland Ltd, The Stock Exchange, London EC2N 1HP.

Previous Editions by the Author

Stocks and Shares Simplified (3rd edn), ISBN 0-471-92131-9, published by John Wiley & Sons Ltd, Chichester.

Traded Options Simplified (1st edn), ISBN 1-871857-00-7, published by Qudos Publications, distributed by John Wiley & Sons Ltd, Chichester.

Channel Analysis (1st edn), ISBN 1-871857-02-3, published by Qudos Publications, distributed by John Wiley & Sons Ltd, Chichester.

Winning on the Stock Market (1st edn), ISBN 0-471-93881-5, published by John Wiley & Sons Ltd, Chichester.

Profitable Charting Techniques (1st edn), ISBN 1-871857-03-1, published by Qudos Publications, distributed by John Wiley & Sons Ltd, Chichester.

Chart Books

Chart books of the alpha shares and others are obtainable from Qudos Publications Ltd, PO Box 27, Bramhall, Stockport, Cheshire SK7 1JH. Tel: 0161-439-3926, Fax: 0161-439-2327.

Historical Data

Closing prices of all alpha shares since 1983 are obtainable in printed form or on floppy disk in a variety of formats from Qudos Publications Ltd.

Microcomputer Software

The charts in this book were produced by the Microvest 5.0 and Sigma-p packages, published by Qudos Publications Ltd.

Index